Praise for *Global Mindset*

"This book is full of helpful strategies and important considerations to get you thinking—I wish I would have had it twelve years ago when I established my first international office. Highly recommend for anyone who does business internationally!"

– Josh Steimle, CEO of the marketing agency MWI and founder of Published Author

"To lead successfully in the global era, a local mindset, a local skill set, and a local MBA don't cut it. You need a new tool kit, and that tool kit is this book. Steve and Bryan have learned the hard lessons of cross-cultural management so you don't have to. Read and lead!"

– Andrew Salmon, Asia Editor at *The Washington Times*

"*Global Mindset* is a must read for international business people. Success in multicultural business settings isn't as easy as it may seem—this book will give you new insights and provide strategies to help you succeed. Through my personal business interactions with Steve, I've gained great respect and admiration for his expertise and his ability to connect with people. Steve and Bryan are great examples of leading with a global mindset, and this book gives you the opportunity to be mentored by them."

– David Rodrigo Fernández Esquivel, CEO and cofounder of the Virtual Advisory Board, London, England

"It is a pleasure to now have Steve and Bryan McKinney's vast experience laid out in *Global Mindset*, which sheds light on fundamental topics with a blend of cross-cultural research and real-world case studies. In a rapidly changing world, the skills presented herein are more relevant than ever."

– Heather A. Willoughby, professor at the Graduate School of International Studies, Ewha Womans University, Seoul, Korea

"This book is a powerhouse of theory and case stories, a wizard's book filled with spells ready for real-life use, and a compass guiding you through cultural differences. An eye-opening treasure trove of knowledge. A truly essential book in today's world, where cross-cultural understanding is crucial for operating in the 'global village.' Thank you for providing insight, theory, and practically usable case stories, all in one!"

– Peter Strandgaard, chief legal officer at FairWind, Netherlands

"*Global Mindset* does an outstanding job of covering the complex world of cross-cultural communications as well as global branding, marketing, and supply chains. For those involved in the global marketplace, this book offers an insightful way of navigating international business issues and concerns in a practical and proactive manner."

– Bryan E. Hopkins, author of *The Art of Legal Risk Management* and *Legal Risk Management for In-House Counsel and Managers*

"To succeed in today's demanding business world, having a global mindset is now a basic tenet for any manager. I have known Steve McKinney for nearly thirty years, and his insight and knowledge on this topic is second to none. I highly recommend reading and adhering to his insights."

– Brad Buckwalter, board member at SK Shieldus

"*Global Mindset* is an essential resource for leaders navigating today's globalized world. In a time when business seamlessly transcends borders, this insightful guide serves as a compass for mastering cross-cultural leadership. Drawing from rich personal experiences, real-world examples, and practical case studies, the authors demonstrate how cultural awareness can transform potential conflicts into opportunities for synergy. Beyond explaining the significance of a global mindset, the book offers actionable strategies to build trust, enhance communication, and drive innovation across cultural divides."

– Sean Garrick, head of the Yongsan International School of Seoul

"*Global Mindset* is an indispensable resource for thriving as an impactful cross-cultural leader. Steve and Bryan McKinney masterfully distill decades of international experience into actionable principles, technical expertise, and engaging real-world case studies. This book equips readers to become trust builders, effective communicators, and innovative problem solvers in our interconnected global landscape."

– Michael K. Chin, regional chair of the Asia Pacific Virtual Advisory Board

"In a highly globalized world, developing a global mindset brings unique opportunities and challenges that grow us as individuals. Steve and Bryan have written a clear, practical introduction to the benefits and realities of intercultural leadership based on deep knowledge of the topic. An invaluable addition to your business tool kit!"

– Alanna Clegg, global strategy advisor

"Whether you are contemplating entering international business or already have a few years of overseas experience, you would do well to pick up this book. Steve and Bryan McKinney have distilled into words what it takes to be successful in this arena."

– Eric Thorpe, founding and managing partner
of Edge Communications, Seoul, Korea

"Steve's upbeat and engaging personality, which makes every project he touches a success, is reflected in the accessible and impactful writing of this book. As an accomplished tenor and conductor, Steve understands the power of harmonizing diverse elements to create a unified whole. He and Bryan have demystified the concept of a global mindset, providing leaders with a clear road map to building culturally intelligent teams and fostering international collaboration. Much like how the blending of a choir can bridge emotional divides, this book harmonizes diverse cultural perspectives into a unified approach. This is a must-read for anyone seeking to lead effectively across cultures."

– Dr. Ryan Goessl, CEO of Korea Concert Tours;
music link and artistic director at Camarata Music

"I wholeheartedly endorse Steve and Bryan McKinney's latest book as a must-read for anyone aspiring to step onto the global stage. This book offers a no-nonsense approach, packed with genuine, proven tips and insights that are essential for young, globally minded individuals and seasoned professionals taking on greater responsibilities beyond their home markets. Their insights are impressive and invaluable for anyone looking to thrive in a global environment. This is undoubtedly one of the best books I have encountered on the subject. I only wish I had it in hand years ago as I embarked on my own global journey!"

– David Houser, global CRO, EVP, advisor, investor,
and fractional executive

"*Global Mindset* is a powerful, practical guide for busy professionals who may have little international experience but recognize the need to lead with clarity, empathy, and confidence. Drawing on decades of hands-on global leadership, Steve and Bryan McKinney offer a road map that's both deeply human and immediately actionable. This book will change how you think, lead, and succeed in a globalized world."

– Michael Sneddon, international entrepreneur and CEO at JSK Therapeutics

"Few books marry elegance and pragmatism as effortlessly as *Global Mindset*. Its insights into cross-cultural leadership and global strategy come with the gravitas of hard-won experience, offering a blueprint that is both urbane in wisdom and razor-sharp in delivering strategic value."

– Brian M. Harris, independent director at LOTTE Hotels & Resorts; president of USO South Korea

"There are many misconceptions about the challenges in establishing and leading the development of international offices, and not much has been written about this in general. It is refreshing to see this new book that presents a tool kit for the aspiring leader looking to step boldly into the challenges presented. Having had this experience myself, I can say that this book is a must-read for such leaders."

– John Walker AM, chairman at Eastpoint Partners

"Having known Steve and Bryan for over two decades, I've witnessed their deep understanding of the global business landscape firsthand. This book isn't just theory; it's a practical tool kit forged from years of real-world experience. Their insights on developing a global mindset are invaluable in today's complex, interconnected world. This book is a must-read for any leader serious about navigating the future."

– Scott Oleson, Deloitte Korea partner

"The skill set laid out in *Global Mindset* is crucial to success in today's interconnected world, driving as it does progress in both business and society. This comprehensive and practical book should be essential reading for all those who work with or who have plans to work with people all over the world."

– Michael Jenkins, CEO of Expert Humans, partner at Future Work Forum, and author of *Expert Humans* and *Toxic Humans*

GLOBAL MINDSET

A GUIDE FOR Cross-Cultural Leadership

Steve McKinney

Bryan McKinney

www.amplifypublishing.com

Global Mindset: A Guide for Cross-Cultural Leadership

©2026 Steve & Bryan McKinney. All Rights Reserved. No part of this publication may be reproduced, stored in a retrieval system or transmitted in any form by any means electronic, mechanical, or photocopying, recording or otherwise without the permission of the author.

For more information, please contact:
Amplify Publishing, an imprint of Amplify Publishing Group
620 Herndon Parkway, Suite 220
Herndon, VA 20170
info@amplifypublishing.com

Library of Congress Control Number: 2025919153

CPSIA Code: PRV1125A

ISBN-13: 979-8-89138-979-3

Printed in the United States

To Jeong-Ok McKinney:

We dedicate this book to you for your selfless daily sacrifice for us. This book could not have been written without your support. We are better men because of you.

SM & BM

CONTENTS

Introduction i

Section 1: Foundations of a Global Mindset

Chapter 1: The Benefits of a Global Mindset 1
Chapter 2: How to Develop a Global Mindset 13
Chapter 3: Key Traits of a Global Leader 25

Section 2: Doing Business Across Cultures

Chapter 4: Cross-Cultural Communication 35
Chapter 5: Intercultural Conflict Resolution 51
Chapter 6: Navigating In-Group and Out-Group Dynamics 63
Chapter 7: Attracting, Retaining, and Cultivating Talent 73
Chapter 8: Navigating Ethics in a Globalized World 83
Chapter 9: Global Supply Chain Management 91
Chapter 10: Global Marketing and Branding 99
Chapter 11: Emerging Markets 111

Section 3: Innovation

Chapter 12: The Digital Transformation of Global Business.....127
Chapter 13: Fueling Creativity in a Connected World..............151
Chapter 14: Global Entrepreneurship..157

Section 4: Case Studies and Future Perspectives

Chapter 15: Global Mindset Leader Case Studies.......................167
Chapter 16: The Future of Global Business.................................179
Conclusion: A Global Perspective..187

Acknowledgments...191
Bibliography...193
Recommended Resources...197
About the Authors...199

INTRODUCTION

Do you lead, or desire to lead, a multicultural team, whether at home or abroad? Do you want to become proficient at navigating the challenges that inevitably arise as you do so? In this book we share what we have learned over the course of decades working in global leadership to guide you through the process of becoming a successful intercultural leader, able to maintain a global mindset while leading diverse teams across cultures. We share technical knowledge and exclusive case studies that demonstrate intercultural leadership practices to guide you in your journey.

Successful intercultural leaders are sensitive to differences across various cultures and are agile and adaptable as they lead diverse teams. They navigate cultural nuances, bridge communication gaps, and foster a sense of belonging among team members from diverse backgrounds. By understanding, respecting, and appreciating cultural differences, they inspire and motivate teams to achieve shared goals. They create inclusive work environments where individuals from diverse backgrounds feel valued and empowered to contribute their unique perspectives and strengths.

This book will serve as your guidepost on the path to becoming a truly impactful cross-cultural leader. Within these pages, you will discover the wisdom and insights necessary to navigate the complexities of leading diverse teams effectively to achieve remarkable results. You will gain a profound understanding of cultural nuances, communication styles, and leadership strategies, empowering you to build high-performing teams, foster inclusivity, and drive innovation in a globalized world.

OUR GLOBAL LEADERSHIP EXPERIENCE

Steve

From 1980 to 1984, when serving in the US military, I spent time in South Korea, Scotland, and Panama. This work among people from other cultures during my early adulthood inspired me to pursue international opportunities in the years that followed.

In 1990 I began managing Reebok International's largest manufacturing facility in the world—a 5,000-employee operation in Busan, South Korea that produced 14.4 million pairs of footwear annually. I then directed Reebok's main product development center located in South Korea. And from 1994 to 1996, I was the head of global product development for Adidas International, headquartered in the US. In this role I led and collaborated with teams in China, Germany, Hong Kong, Indonesia, Korea, Taiwan, and Thailand.

In 2001 I established McKinney Consulting, an executive search and leadership consulting practice based in Seoul. We've placed hundreds of middle- to senior-level executives in Fortune 500 companies throughout Asia. We've conducted executive and cross-cultural coaching and start-up CEO coaching for hundreds of multinational company leaders from more than thirty different countries.

From 2003 to 2013 I served as a board member and then as an advisor to the American Chamber of Commerce in South Korea. For three years I oversaw the Seoul Global Center (SGC) for the Seoul Metropolitan Government—the largest foreign residence support organization in the world. The SGC consisted of four Global Business Centers, seven Migrant Workers Centers, and seven Global Village Centers.

Currently, I also serve on multiple boards, including the Korea Foreign Schools Foundation, whose member organizations include the Korea Ministry of Commerce, the Seoul Metropolitan Government, the Seoul Chamber of Commerce, and the Korean Chamber of Commerce. I also serve on the Institute Council for Kestria (the world's largest executive search alliance) and the Asia Pacific Council for the Association of Executive Search Consultants. I am currently the South Korea county chair for the Virtual Advisory Board.

Bryan

I have more than twelve years of leadership experience at McKinney Consulting in Seoul, serving in operations, coaching, and executive search roles. I have also served on selection committees for private companies and government entities.

From 2014 to 2016 I headed up AfreecaTV Co.'s expansion into the USA. AfreecaTV Co. (now SOOP) is a Korean technology company that provides an interactive platform that allows users to stream, watch videos, and socially interact with people from around the world. It is used by many idol groups to interact with their fans.

Since 2017 I have represented McKinney Consulting in our Kestria global executive search partner alliance interactions. I am also the program director and master certified coach for the Success Factor Coaching program.

I have lived and worked in Hawaii, Japan, Korea, and various cities in the US. I am a native English speaker and am also fluent in Korean and Japanese.

Over the years, we have learned a lot about how to be successful intercultural leaders, and we're excited to share what we've learned with you in the chapters that follow.

Applying the principles discussed in this book will exponentially increase your odds of success as a global leader.

We wish you all the best in your intercultural leadership journey!

Steve McKinney and Bryan McKinney

Disclaimer:

Throughout this book we explore various cultural dimensions. These are generalizations and should not be used to stereotype or judge individuals or cultures. It is crucial to remember that culture is a complex and multifaceted phenomenon, and individual behaviors and beliefs vary significantly within any given culture.

Furthermore, cultural dimensions are not static; they evolve over time due to various factors such as globalization, modernization, and social change. Therefore, it is essential to approach cultural differences with an open mind, curiosity, and a willingness to learn and adapt.

SECTION 1

FOUNDATIONS OF A GLOBAL MINDSET

Chapter 1

THE BENEFITS OF A GLOBAL MINDSET

When I (Steve) began working internationally in the 1980s, I was utterly unprepared for the cultural challenges I would encounter. Although cross-cultural psychology had emerged as a distinct field of study in the late 1960s, many businesspeople were unaware of its significance. It is no longer possible to disregard cultural differences when doing business internationally—in today's interconnected world, understanding cultural differences and thinking and acting with a global mindset are absolutely essential for successful intercultural business collaboration.

WHAT IS A GLOBAL MINDSET?

Developing an international perspective—a global mindset—means increasing your cultural awareness and being able to understand and appreciate people from different cultures. It means having the ability to see the world from multiple perspectives and appreciate the interconnectedness of cultures. It is characterized by being open to new ideas and willing to learn from others. It also means adapting one's thinking and behavior to other cultural contexts when doing so is prudent.

As you develop a global mindset and become more aware of diverse cultures and their customs, you will be able to avoid cultural blunders and build stronger relationships. Rather than viewing cultural differences as a source of conflict, you'll recognize that they can provide an opportunity for synergy.

WHAT WE MEAN BY "CULTURE"

Culture is a collective system of distinct beliefs, values, customs, behaviors, and artifacts. We each interpret our experiences, guide our actions, and solve problems based on our culture. So when encountering a problem, the solutions presented by one culture could easily differ from those offered by a different culture.

Some components of culture, such as clothing, food, art, sports, and language, are easy to identify, while other factors, such as body language, education, law, politics, religious and other beliefs, values, vision of the world, etc., are not as easy to distinguish between cultures. However, as you learn about cultural differences and develop a global mindset, you will better recognize and appreciate these cultural differences. You'll better understand the various ways that people from different cultures communicate, the diverse values and beliefs that people from various cultures hold, and the different customs and traditions that people from diverse cultures observe.

BENEFITS OF A GLOBAL MINDSET

We'll discuss later *how* to develop a global mindset. But first, *why* should you put in the effort? What are the benefits of having a global mindset?

There are many, but we will focus on the benefits of forming relationships of trust, improved communication skills, enhanced problem-solving skills, personal enrichment, and increased business opportunities and job security.

Forming Relationships of Trust

When you approach every multicultural or international interaction with a global mindset and an open mind, it will maximize your ability to understand the other person, establish trust, and build a meaningful relationship.

Cultivating trust in intercultural relationships requires patience and consistent effort. It involves demonstrating genuine interest in the other person's culture, listening to their perspective, and showing respect for their values and beliefs. Be open and honest in your interactions, acknowledge your own cultural biases, and be willing to learn from others. Engage in activities that foster social interaction and build rapport, such as shared meals, social events, or cultural exchange programs. Consistent and reliable behavior builds trust over time. Follow through on your commitments and demonstrate that you can be relied upon.

Improved Communication

Operating with a global mindset increases understanding and appreciation of different cultures and thus leads to improved communication.

Understanding how different cultures communicate (discussed in greater length in chapter 4) helps us achieve our goals and ambitions more effectively.

Indeed, cultivating a global mindset allows us to bridge cultural divides and foster deeper understanding. This enhanced communication not only strengthens personal and professional relationships but also contributes to a more harmonious and interconnected global society.

Consider international business negotiations: In some cultures, building rapport through small talk and relationship-building is paramount, while in others, direct and efficient communication is valued. Having a global mindset will help you avoid making common cultural faux pas such as:

- making direct eye contact in a culture where such eye contact is considered rude
- giving gifts that are considered inappropriate in a particular culture
- using humor in situations where it is not culturally appropriate

By understanding these nuances, we can navigate these delicate waters with grace and achieve mutually beneficial outcomes.

Enhanced Problem-Solving Skills

A global mindset cultivates a multifaceted perspective, enabling us to view challenges through a kaleidoscope of lenses. By understanding the diverse ways in which different cultures approach and solve problems, we gain valuable insights and develop more creative and effective solutions. For example, a team tackling a complex design challenge comprised of individuals from various cultural backgrounds may bring forth unique perspectives, drawing upon diverse cultural experiences and problem-solving techniques. This cross-pollination of ideas can lead to innovative solutions that would not have been possible within a more homogenous environment.

Moreover, the ability to synthesize these varied viewpoints enhances our analytical skills, enabling us to dissect problems with greater precision and depth. It is this very essence of leveraging diverse ideas that transforms conventional problem-solving into a dynamic and enriched process. By embracing a global mindset, we not only elevate our capacity for innovation but also foster a collaborative spirit that transcends borders and unites us in our quest for excellence.

The following case study helps illustrate the importance of a global mindset in cross-cultural collaboration.

CASE STUDY: GLOBAL MINDSET FOR IMPROVED INTERNATIONAL RELATIONS

The Role of Free Trade Agreements in Globalization

Free trade agreements (FTAs) have been pivotal in fostering economic globalization by reducing trade barriers, promoting market access, and encouraging investment. The North American Free Trade Agreement (NAFTA), the Trans-Pacific Partnership (TPP), and the Korea–United States Free Trade Agreement (KORUS FTA) are notable examples of these agreements that have facilitated cross-border trade and investment.

Navigating Cross-Cultural Challenges in the KORUS FTA

As a board member of the American Chamber of Commerce–Korea, I (Steve) had the opportunity to participate in discussions surrounding the implementation of the KORUS FTA. During an advisory session with a senior White House official, we explored several cross-cultural issues that arose during the negotiation process.

One such issue was South Korea's reluctance to purchase high-quality short-grain rice from California despite the significantly lower price compared to domestic production. This seemingly irrational behavior was rooted in cultural and historical factors, as rice is a staple food in Korea and there was a strong preference for domestic production due to concerns about food security.

Another challenge related to cultural differences was the perception of equality and fairness. While the Americans were eager to open their vast market to South Korea, Korean businesses and government officials were concerned they would not be treated equally by their American counterparts. This disparity in perception was rooted in the two countries' differing cultural values and expectations.

Building Trust Through Cultural Understanding and Concrete Actions

To overcome these challenges and foster a successful partnership, I emphasized the importance of cultural understanding and building trust. I suggested to the Americans that the quickest way to connect with Koreans is through their hearts. By demonstrating respect, care, and commitment, they could establish a strong foundation for trust and cooperation.

As a concrete step to demonstrate their commitment, I proposed that the United States grant South Korea entry into the Visa Waiver Program. This would be a significant gesture of goodwill, helping to build trust and strengthen the bilateral relationship. Following this suggestion, the senior White House official secured South Korea's inclusion in the program, paving the way for smoother trade and investment flows.

While free trade agreements offer numerous benefits, they also present challenges related to cultural differences, language barriers, and time zone differences. By addressing these challenges and fostering a culture of understanding and cooperation, we can maximize the benefits of globalization and create a more interconnected and prosperous world.

CASE STUDY: PROBLEM-SOLVING IN THE GLOBAL ATHLETIC FOOTWEAR INDUSTRY

In the 1990s, I (Steve) had the opportunity to witness firsthand the dynamic nature of global manufacturing. While leading Reebok's largest factory, then while serving as the head of footwear product development for Adidas International, South Korea and Taiwan emerged as global hubs for athletic footwear manufacturing. This strategic shift was driven by a combination of factors, including availability of skilled labor, advanced manufacturing capabilities, and proximity to key markets.

However, as companies were presented with the problem of increasing labor costs in these regions, I witnessed another significant transformation in the industry. Major brands, including Reebok, Adidas, and Nike, sought to reduce costs by relocating their manufacturing operations to countries with lower labor costs, such as China,

Thailand, Indonesia, and Vietnam. This shift necessitated a global mindset from those managing these factories, requiring leaders to adapt to new cultural contexts, navigate complex supply chains, and manage diverse teams.

By operating in various countries, I and other leaders gained invaluable experience in understanding cultural nuances, building relationships with diverse stakeholders, and developing effective cross-cultural communication strategies.

The global perspective I gained enabled me to solve problems, identify opportunities for innovation, and improve continuously. For instance, when faced with supply chain disruptions caused by natural disasters and geopolitical events, a global mindset allowed me to explore alternative sourcing options and implement contingency plans. By analyzing the root causes of these disruptions and identifying potential risks, we were able to mitigate the impact on our business.

Furthermore, a global mindset helped me address problems related to sustainability and ethical sourcing. By working with suppliers in different regions, I gained a deeper understanding of the social and environmental challenges faced by the industry. This knowledge enabled us to implement more sustainable practices such as reducing waste, minimizing our carbon footprint, and promoting fair labor standards.

The global athletic footwear industry serves as a compelling example of the benefits of a global mindset. By embracing diversity, adapting to change, and fostering innovation, leaders can navigate the complexities of a globalized world and drive sustainable growth.

Personal Enrichment

A global mindset is more than just a professional asset; it's personally enriching. Cultivating a global perspective broadens your horizons and deepens your understanding of the world. Traveling and living abroad allows you to enjoy different cultures as you experience their unique customs, traditions, and cuisines. Interacting with people from other countries can lead to lifelong friendships and professional networks. By cultivating a global mindset, you unlock a world of possibilities and live a more fulfilling and enriching life.

Increased Career Opportunities and Job Security

Years ago, when I (Steve) served in the US military and was sent on missions and training exercises in South Korea, Panama, and Scotland, little did I realize how much this exposure to other cultures would affect my future career. These intercultural experiences in my early adulthood helped start me on the path of developing a global mindset and helped me be open to and ready for future international career opportunities.

Is a global mindset necessary for your business career? In this ever-changing global environment, we think the answer is yes. Today's job market is dynamic and unpredictable, demanding versatility and a willingness to embrace new opportunities. Numerous studies have shown that individuals with international experience demonstrate enhanced adaptability, cultural sensitivity, and problem-solving skills—highly valued qualities in today's globalized workplace.

Individuals who have international work experience often possess a deeper understanding of global markets, intercultural communication, and diverse perspectives. This broader perspective makes them more valuable assets to organizations, increasing their employability and career advancement potential. For example, during economic downturns, individuals with a global mindset and international experience may be more likely to retain employment due to their unique skill sets and adaptability in navigating complex and uncertain environments.

By understanding different cultures and business practices, individuals can adapt to changing circumstances and seize opportunities in a globalized economy. This adaptability and flexibility are highly valued by employers, making individuals with a global mindset more competitive in the job market. Moreover, a global mindset enables individuals to identify and implement best practices from around the world, leading to increased efficiency and innovation. By sharing knowledge and experiences across borders, global-minded individuals can contribute to the success of their organizations and advance their own careers.

A global mindset will help you access new markets and customers in your career. Better relationships with people from all over the world have distinct advantages. A deeper understanding of different cultures allows for more creativity and innovative ideas to materialize. All these help in the decision-making process.

Our executive search practice, which places middle- to senior-level executives for multinational companies in Korea, doesn't consider candidates unless they have already worked for a multinational company and are bilingual. All other factors being equal, the person with a global mindset and more international experience will have a better chance of being hired. Other multinational companies have similar preferences as they seek to recruit talent for their companies.

When it comes to international companies making decisions regarding hiring, promotions, and retention during layoffs, those employees who have a global mindset will have a definite advantage over those who do not.

KEY TAKEAWAYS

A global mindset offers numerous benefits for individuals and organizations in today's interconnected world. Developing a global mindset leads to stronger relationships, improved communication and problem-solving skills, personal enrichment, and increased career opportunities and job security.

Reflect on your organization's global mindset—how well do your leaders and employees maintain an international perspective? What are your organization's strengths and weaknesses? How can you improve your organization's global mindset?

Chapter 2

HOW TO DEVELOP A GLOBAL MINDSET

Cultivating a global mindset is a lifelong pursuit, a continuous journey of exploration and self-discovery. How does one go about changing their perspective so they understand and appreciate other cultures? How does one become a leader who thinks and acts globally? First, we'll tell you about Steve's experience.

STEVE'S JOURNEY TO DEVELOPING A GLOBAL MINDSET

My journey toward a global mindset began in the vibrant tapestry of childhood as I traveled with my family's Southern gospel singing group across the diverse landscape of the eastern part of the United States. These early experiences, steeped in the collective joy of music and the profound connection with diverse audiences, instilled within me a deep appreciation for the shared humanity of people from different cultures. They helped me realize early on that there are many ways to see and approach the world, that the existence of different cultures creates a rich human experience.

During early adulthood, my US military service further broadened my horizons, immersing me in diverse cultures. Deployments to Scotland, South Korea, and Panama exposed me to a treasure trove of human experiences, from life in the rugged beauty of the Scottish Highlands to the vibrant mosaic of life in the Panamanian jungle. My time in South Korea, in particular, left an indelible mark, introducing me to the unique blend of ancient traditions and cutting-edge technology that defines this dynamic nation.

Serving alongside fellow soldiers from a variety of races and cultures—Puerto Rican, Mexican, Italian, German, Korean, Black, White, and many others—fostered a profound respect for the unique perspectives and experiences that shape each individual. My marriage to a South Korean woman further enriched this tapestry, weaving into my life new traditions and customs and a deeper understanding of the Korean spirit.

Later, working for global athletic footwear giants like Reebok and Adidas provided invaluable opportunities for international travel, collaboration, and cultural immersion. Engaging with colleagues and clients across Asia, Europe, and the United States, I learned to navigate the intricate dance of diverse business cultures, adapting my communication style to resonate with each unique context.

As the head of the Seoul Global Center, I had the privilege of interacting with individuals from more than 100 countries, each a unique thread in the vibrant tapestry of humanity. One particularly memorable experience involved mentoring a young Mexican entrepreneur eager to launch a tech start-up in Seoul. By carefully navigating the cultural nuances of both Korean and Mexican business practices, we were able to identify potential challenges and develop strategies for success.

Through these experiences, I learned that true intercultural understanding requires empathy, active listening, cultural sensitivity, and a genuine curiosity about the human condition. I learned that being open-minded, respectful, and adaptable is essential when working with people from different cultures.

As a result of cultivating a global mindset through these life experiences, I developed the skills and expertise needed to establish McKinney Consulting, which offers executive search and executive coaching to multinational organizations. At McKinney Consulting, every day is a cross-cultural experience.

DEVELOPING A GLOBAL MINDSET

Developing a global mindset begins with a profound appreciation for the inherent diversity of human experience, recognizing that our own cultural lens, while valuable, offers but a single perspective on the vast and intricate tapestry of human existence. Through introspection and a willingness to challenge our own assumptions, we can begin to dismantle the barriers of our own cultural conditioning.

Here are some specific ways you can develop a global mindset.

Recognize Your Own Cultural Values

Recognizing your own cultural values and biases is a crucial first step in developing a global mindset. Often we are so deeply ingrained in our culture that we take our beliefs, behaviors, and assumptions for granted. We are like fish in water, unaware of the fluid that surrounds us and the forces shaping us. By stepping outside of our comfort zone and engaging with people from different cultures, we can begin to identify our cultural values and blind spots and develop a more nuanced understanding of the world.

If you are from an individualistic culture, you may prioritize personal achievement and independence, while those from collectivist cultures may value group harmony and interdependence. For a discussion about many other values that vary between cultures, see chapter 8.

Understanding differences in values among cultures helps us avoid misunderstandings, build stronger relationships, and work more effectively with people from diverse backgrounds.

Be Humble and Open to Other Cultures

Cultivating a global mindset begins with a deep sense of humility. Recognize that your own cultural background, values, and experiences provide only one perspective on the world. Be open to learning from others, acknowledging that your own assumptions and beliefs may not be universally applicable or the only right way to see the world. Accept the opportunity to learn from the perspectives of others and challenge your own assumptions.

True intercultural understanding requires a willingness to step outside your comfort zone and embrace the unfamiliar. We must approach each interaction with a spirit of inquiry, recognizing that every individual carries within them a unique worldview shaped by their own cultural experiences, history, and social context. By acknowledging our own limitations and approaching each encounter with humility and a genuine desire to learn, we create a space for meaningful dialogue and foster deeper connections across cultural boundaries.

Learn About Cultural Nuances in Communication Styles

Cultural differences significantly impact communication styles and expectations. For instance, many Western cultures value open and direct communication. People may express their opinions freely and engage in debates. However, more indirect communication styles are preferred in some Eastern cultures, such as in Japan and Korea. Explicit disagreement or criticism may be considered impolite or disrespectful in these cultures.

Additionally, the role of silence varies across cultures. In Western cultures, long pauses in conversation may be interpreted as awkward or a sign of disinterest. In contrast, in some Eastern cultures, silence is a powerful tool for communication, conveying respect, contemplation, or disagreement.

By understanding cultural nuances in communication, individuals can avoid misunderstandings and build stronger relationships with people from diverse backgrounds.

CASE STUDY: THE IMPORTANCE OF COMMUNICATION SENSITIVITY

A foreign manager's criticism of a worker on a South Korean production line led to a significant cultural misunderstanding. When the exchange took place, the manager was accompanied by a group of Korean supervisors, including that worker's supervisor. The foreign manager was very direct in his communication with the worker, but South Koreans favor an indirect approach. While the foreign manager may have intended only to provide feedback, his behavior was interpreted more harshly by the Korean supervisors. The worker's Korean supervisor fired her the next day.

The foreign manager could have avoided this cultural misunderstanding by using a culturally appropriate indirect approach and waiting until he was away from the production line and away from the group of supervisors to discuss the quality issue with the worker.

This experience underscores the importance of leaders fostering productive and respectful workplace relationships by communicating in culturally appropriate ways and learning from their mistakes. Chapter 4 discusses cultural differences in communication in greater detail.

Learn About Business Etiquette Rules

There are many cultural differences in workplace expectations across the globe. For example, in some East Asian cultures, the meeting leader holds a position of authority and controls the agenda. Staff members are generally expected to remain silent unless specifically called upon to provide input. Deviating from this protocol may be considered disrespectful and result in negative consequences. In contrast, in some other cultures, staff members are expected to contribute during meetings and silence may be interpreted as disinterest or a lack of investment in the meeting and its outcomes.

By becoming aware of such expectations in the countries where you do business, you can avoid misunderstandings and build stronger relationships. Business etiquette is discussed in greater detail in chapter 4.

Seek Out Intercultural Experiences and Build Solid Intercultural Relationships

If we spend time only with people from our own culture, it is more difficult to develop a global mindset. Being intentional about networking and building relationships with people from different cultures helps us in our effort to see the world with a global mindset. Firsthand experiences, such as through travel and cultural exchange programs, are invaluable in cultivating a global mindset. By immersing oneself in new cultures, interacting with people from diverse backgrounds, and experiencing the world through different lenses, we broaden our horizons, challenge our assumptions, and develop a deeper understanding of our interconnected world.

To build intercultural relationships while living in your home country, you can seek out holiday celebrations or other events that celebrate the traditions of a specific country. Seeking out authentic international restaurants is another good way to learn about other cultures and meet people from those cultures.

If you live in or visit a foreign country, travelling around and exploring that country is a great way to show genuine interest in the people and culture. It's fun to visit touristy spots, but for greater insights into a culture, seek out sites, experiences, and restaurants frequented by locals. As you do so, be observant. For example, being observant while eating at a restaurant in Asia, you may notice that the rice bowl is traditionally placed on the left and that you should not begin eating until after the oldest person present begins. Being curious and asking questions shows interest in your host country and people.

Another great way to form relationships with people from other cultures is to find people with a common interest. It may be a language skill, a hobby, a sport, an interest in the same food, or anything that will help establish a relationship.

As you interact with people from other cultures, look for the strengths of their culture and the advantages to doing things the way they do, be flexible, and be willing to share your own culture with them.

Participate in Global Mindset Training Programs

Seeking out global mindset training programs is another way to cultivate a global mindset. Many companies offer these programs to their employees, and some universities and professional development organizations provide training to the general public.

Cultural sensitivity training, for instance, provides a valuable framework for understanding the subtle nuances of cross-cultural communication. Through engaging in activities such as role-playing scenarios and cultural simulations, participants gain a deeper appreciation for the impact of cultural values and beliefs on human interaction. These experiences foster empathy and equip individuals with the tools to navigate intercultural encounters with greater sensitivity and grace.

Cross-cultural communication workshops equip individuals with the practical skills necessary to navigate the complexities of communication across diverse cultural landscapes. By focusing on verbal and nonverbal communication styles, active listening, and conflict resolution strategies, these workshops empower individuals to communicate effectively and build bridges of understanding across cultural divides.

Unconscious bias training provides a structured framework for raising awareness and fostering critical self-reflection regarding the subtle influences of unconscious biases on decision-making processes. By exploring the nature of these biases and their potential impact on workplace dynamics, these training programs empower employees to recognize and mitigate their biases, contributing to a more equitable organizational culture.

Immersing oneself in a new language through *language learning programs* offers a unique window into another culture. By engaging with the nuances of a new language, we begin to understand the underlying cultural values, beliefs, and perspectives that shape its expression. This journey of linguistic exploration not only enhances our communication skills but also deepens our appreciation for the richness and diversity of human thought and expression.

Finally, *global leadership development programs* provide a unique platform for cultivating global leadership skills. Through immersive experiences such as global team projects and simulations of international business operations, participants gain invaluable insights into the challenges and opportunities of leading diverse teams in an interconnected world. These programs foster collaboration, enhance intercultural competence, and equip leaders with the tools they need to thrive in a globalized environment.

This holistic approach to cultivating a global mindset is mirrored in organizational strategies, such as Mars Incorporated's Global Talent Development Program, which provides employees with immersive international experiences. This initiative empowers employees to engage in international projects, collaborate with diverse teams, and gain invaluable cross-cultural experiences. By cultivating a global mindset, Mars is building a dynamic and skilled workforce capable of driving innovation and growth in today's increasingly interconnected marketplace.

We recently coached a multinational luxury automotive company leader participating in a fast-track leadership program aimed at helping him develop a global mindset. His first assignment was to work for six months in Germany. Next, he worked in the Netherlands for nine months, South Korea for nine months, and finally, the US for six months.

This type of global mindset leadership training in various cultures was invaluable to his company but also invaluable to him personally. He learned how to embrace challenges in different cultures and developed a constant desire to learn and improve. He will now be more agile and adaptable when dealing with people in other cultures, both in his current role and any future roles.

HOW LONG DOES IT TAKE TO DEVELOP A GLOBAL MINDSET?

Developing a global mindset is an ongoing process that takes time, effort, and commitment. But it is worth the investment. How long it will take depends on several factors, such as personal experiences and willingness to learn and change. However, most experts agree that developing a global mindset takes years of experience and practice. So it's best to get started today! As the Chinese proverb says, "A journey of a thousand miles begins with a single step."

Every effort you make to understand people from other cultures will enrich and benefit your life, so don't be discouraged, however slow the process.

KEY TAKEAWAYS

As you take steps to understand your own cultural values, humble yourself and open yourself to the cultures of others, develop a better understanding of cultural nuances in communication styles, learn about business etiquette in different cultures, seek out intercultural experiences, build intercultural relationships, and participate in global mindset training, you'll be well on your way to developing a global mindset.

Reflect on your organization's global mindset development efforts. What are your strengths and weaknesses? What actions can you take to help your employees develop a global mindset?

Chapter 3

KEY TRAITS OF A GLOBAL LEADER

Consider a man or woman who has achieved remarkable success as a leader within their own homogeneous business community, but has never experienced life beyond a limited geographical radius. Imagine plopping them into a leadership team of individuals from several other countries. Though undoubtedly a capable leader in their familiar context, this individual would face a steep learning curve in the new environment. Their prior lack of exposure to different cultures has likely hindered their understanding of diverse communication styles, how to build trust in a multicultural setting, and how to effectively manage a team that is global.

This scenario illustrates how even the most accomplished leaders must broaden their horizons to succeed in a global context. As business leaders pursue extensive international experience and work to develop a global mindset, they develop a unique blend of qualities and skills that allow them to navigate cultural complexities and lead effectively in an interconnected world.

The exposure to diverse cultures fosters a deep *self-awareness*, which helps leaders understand their biases and assumptions. And it becomes apparent which skills are strengths and which need improvement.

By encountering diverse perspectives and experiences, global leaders develop *tolerance* and *empathy*—the ability to understand and share the feelings of others. This is important for building relationships with people from different cultures, as it allows leaders to see things from another perspective. International experience fosters *cultural awareness and sensitivity*, which becomes a way of life, a way of thinking, and a way of being.

This sensitivity brings with it a companion, *humility*. Humility helps leaders acknowledge their own shortcomings and be *open to learning* from others, both of which are essential for success in a globalized world. This humility allows leaders to remain *adaptable* and *receptive to new ideas and perspectives.*

Cross-cultural leaders also develop an approach that blends *collaboration*, *accommodation*, and sometimes *avoidance* to figure out how to get things done in a new country where their usual approach may not be effective.

The qualities of *curiosity*, *caution*, and *honesty* help global leaders be more effective in problem-solving. Curious leaders constantly seek new information and ideas, eager to expand their understanding of the world. This curiosity fuels their desire to learn from different cultures and perspectives. Curiosity helps leaders identify new opportunities and solutions, while caution helps them avoid making costly mistakes. This balance between seeking and safeguarding is essential for navigating complex global scenarios. If a leader works globally long enough, they will develop a lifelong problem-solving curiosity.

Strategic thinking is another critical skill set for global leaders, which makes it possible for them to analyze complex situations, identify opportunities, and develop effective plans to achieve their goals. The ability to think strategically helps leaders make better decisions about allocating resources and competing in the worldwide marketplace. As they work internationally, their global strategic thinking ability will be enhanced; they have no choice but to improve to survive. They will quickly leave their comfort zone and will adjust and develop the necessary skills required to succeed. The quickest way to fail is to apply outdated methods and strategies to new and unfamiliar cultural contexts. A global mindset helps a leader innovate in foreign cultures, become an early mover in the worldwide marketplace.

Effective communication will help leaders motivate, inspire, and demonstrate understanding and acceptance of the ideas of staff members, clients, and other stakeholders, and also aid in helping them better understand the vision for the future. Global leaders express their thoughts clearly, persuasively, and efficiently. They can also navigate conversations in multiple languages or with the help of a translator.

Other crucial qualities for global leaders are *patience*, *perseverance*, and *optimism*. Working globally often involves dealing with challenges and setbacks. Patience allows leaders to press on through difficulties while remaining optimistic.

This optimism is not blind naivety but rather a belief in the inherent goodness of humanity and the potential for positive change. It is the conviction that, despite the inevitable challenges and setbacks encountered in navigating the complexities of the globalized world, meaningful connections can be forged, mutual understanding can be achieved, and a more just and equitable world can be created.

This optimistic outlook fuels a *proactive* and *solution-oriented approach* to leadership. It empowers leaders to embrace challenges as opportunities for learning and growth, seek innovative solutions to complex problems, and persevere through setbacks with *resilience* and *determination.* It encourages them to view cultural differences not as barriers but as enriching experiences that broaden perspectives and foster creativity.

Furthermore, optimism fosters a sense of *hope* and inspires others. Leaders who exude optimism inspire their teams to embrace new challenges, cultivate a positive and collaborative work environment, and strive for excellence. By cultivating a culture of optimism and encouraging a growth mindset within their teams, leaders help unlock the full potential of their employees and drive innovation and success.

CASE STUDY: THE GLOBAL OPTIMIST

Alex, a young professional from a small town in the United States, was eager to pursue a career in international business. Despite his enthusiasm, Alex often felt overwhelmed by the prospect of working in a foreign country. He worried about language barriers, cultural misunderstandings, and the challenges of adapting to a new way of life.

A turning point came when Alex took a language course and joined a cultural exchange program. Through these experiences, he began to develop a more positive outlook on the challenges of working abroad. He learned to appreciate the diversity of cultures and to embrace new experiences.

Alex's newfound optimism and cheerful attitude helped him overcome his initial fears and develop a global mindset. This mindset has helped him adapt to different cultural contexts, build relationships with people from diverse backgrounds, and thrive in his international career.

One final quality effective global leaders develop is *effective stakeholder management*—these leaders understand the importance of stakeholder management and are able serve many diverse stakeholders in complex environments.

CASE STUDY: THE IMPORTANCE OF EFFECTIVE STAKEHOLDER MANAGEMENT

I (Steve) was recently hired to provide executive coaching to Mark (name changed), a leader from a global company. The challenge, as presented to me at the onset, was perplexing. Mark had various stakeholders from the USA headquarters and several Asian countries. The vice president of human resources told me that, on the one hand, there were leaders in the organization who felt that Mark was on track to be the next CEO of the company. At the same time, some leaders thought that Mark was failing and should be fired. Mark's boss (the senior vice president of the company) and also the vice president of HR liked Mark but didn't know why he was received so differently by different leaders in his company. I was hired by Mark's boss to coach Mark and identify the cause of these evaluation discrepancies.

After a few coaching sessions with Mark, we identified the main root of the problem. Emily (name changed) was a senior leader of similar rank to Mark who worked in a different region. She and Mark reported to the same leader but rarely communicated with each other. Through my interviews with multiple senior leadership team members, I determined that although Emily didn't seem interested in becoming the CEO, she perceived Mark as a threat and viewed him as a competitor. We helped Mark come up with a solution that would help strengthen his relationship with Emily and others within the organization.

We devised a stakeholder management plan that identified Mark's stakeholders, how they like to communicate, and how often he would reach out to each one. This plan worked out perfectly—Mark now has a stronger relationship with Emily and is back on track to becoming the next CEO of the company.

When developing a stakeholder management plan, it's usually clear that some stakeholders, such as direct bosses, dotted-line report lines, and direct reports, should be prominent in the plan. However, as was Mark's situation, we may not recognize that there are often other stakeholders that need to be included.

Mark's case serves as a powerful reminder that effective stakeholder management transcends mere formality, requiring a proactive and nuanced approach. It extends beyond apparent relationships to encompass the subtle dynamics of influence and perception, highlighting the transformative power of understanding and communication in navigating complex organizational landscapes.

Mark's initial challenges stemmed not from a lack of competence but from a failure to recognize and address the underlying perceptions and communication gaps within his network. By meticulously mapping his stakeholders, understanding their communication preferences, and consistently engaging with them through a structured approach, he not only salvaged his career trajectory but also demonstrated the profound impact of tailored communication and genuine connection.

This example underscores the necessity for leaders to cultivate a heightened awareness of their organizational ecosystem, recognizing that even seemingly peripheral connections may significantly impact their influence and advancement. Leadership excellence in today's interconnected world requires not just vision and skill but also emotional intelligence and strategic foresight to build and maintain strong, mutually beneficial relationships with all stakeholders.

KEY TAKEAWAYS

Leading with a global mindset requires a unique combination of skills. By developing the skills discussed in this chapter, leaders can skillfully navigate the complexities of a globalized world and build bridges of cooperation across cultures.

Reflect on your own strengths and weaknesses and the strengths and weaknesses of other leaders in your organization. How can you develop the skills necessary to be more effective as a global leader and help others at your organization do so as well?

SECTION 2

DOING BUSINESS ACROSS CULTURES

Chapter 4

CROSS-CULTURAL COMMUNICATION

Effective communication is the cornerstone of successful intercultural interactions. The way you communicate with those of your own culture may not be as effective with those from other cultures. As a business leader, you must invest time and effort in learning how to communicate effectively with those from the cultures you do business with.

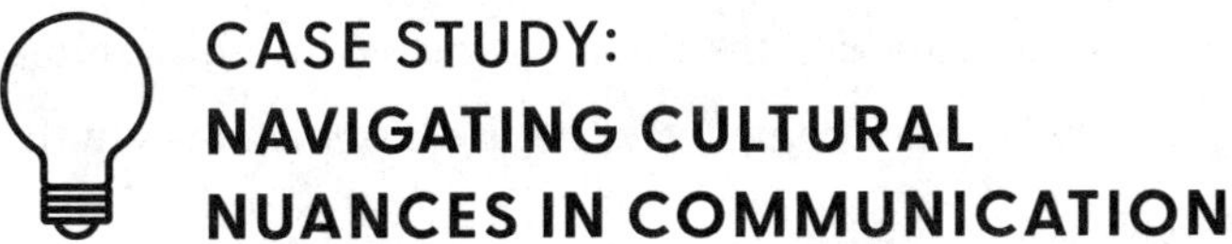

CASE STUDY: NAVIGATING CULTURAL NUANCES IN COMMUNICATION

An American company eager to expand its operations in the Chinese market entered negotiations for a joint venture with a prominent Chinese company. The American negotiators, accustomed to a direct and task-oriented communication approach, were surprised by their Chinese counterparts' seemingly laidback approach.

The Western negotiators struggled to understand the importance of building relationships in Chinese business culture. In Western cultures, business deals are often based on contracts and legal agreements. However, in China, relationships are usually more important than contracts. Building trust and *guanxi* (relationships) is critical in doing business in China.

Another area of confusion for the Western negotiators was the cultural significance of gift-giving in China. In Western cultures, gift-giving is often seen as a gesture of appreciation or friendship. However, in China, gift-giving is a complex social ritual with specific rules and etiquette. Giving and receiving gifts can be a delicate matter, and it is essential to understand the appropriate customs and protocols.

Despite the initial challenges, the Western negotiators learned about and eventually came to understand the Chinese cultural nuances. They adapted their approach to be more patient and indirect—they took the time to build relationships with their Chinese counterparts, and they exchanged gifts appropriately.

The Western negotiators overcame the initial misunderstandings and eventually reached a mutually beneficial business agreement by demonstrating respect for Chinese culture, communicating appropriately, and building trust with their new partners. The joint venture succeeded, and the Western company expanded its operations in the Chinese market.

BUILDING TRUST

While some business interactions are neutral, many either build or break down trust. Here are some tips for building the trust that is essential for successful cross-cultural business relations:

- **Prioritize relationships:** Take the time necessary to establish relationships with your cross-cultural colleagues. Engage in small talk, share personal anecdotes, and express interest in their culture.
- **Listen actively:** During intercultural interactions, listen to what the other party communicates, including with their body language. Show that you are genuinely interested in understanding their perspective by using culturally appropriate eye contact, nodding, and asking clarifying questions.
- **Empathize:** Try to understand the perspective of others, even if it differs from your own.
- **Be honest:** Be transparent in your communication and negotiations. Avoid making false or misleading statements and be willing to compromise when necessary.
- **Be patient:** A little bit of patience and understanding goes a long way when communicating with people from different cultures.

Building trust takes time and effort, but it is a worthwhile investment.

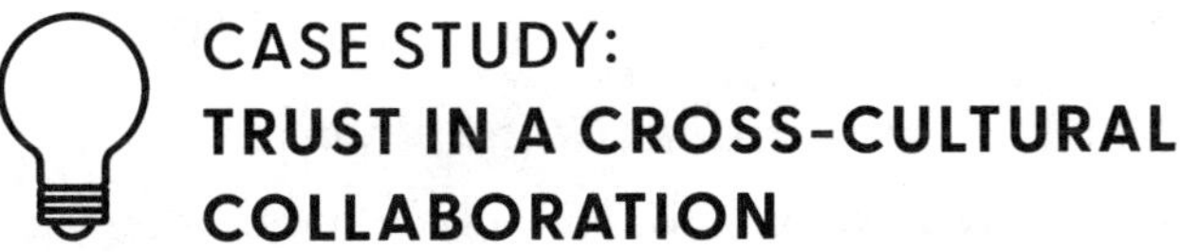

CASE STUDY: TRUST IN A CROSS-CULTURAL COLLABORATION

Nancy (name changed), the Taiwanese president of a contractor factory in Taiwan, asked me (Steve) to meet to discuss our new Converse Actions Sports (athletic footwear) product line. She told me that she and her team liked our best new model for the season and thought it could sell more than 100,000 pairs if we decreased the already agreed upon retail price of the shoe. She proposed making a minor material change to decrease the cost of production so that if we dropped the retail price, I could still maintain my gross margin.

I reviewed the proposed material change and found it to be acceptable. When I discussed Nancy's suggested strategy with my marketing director, he also liked the approach, so we made the deal. The result was an increase in sales from our initial forecast, almost as much as Nancy had predicted.

From the onset of our discussion, Nancy built trust with me by being honest and transparent about her goals, demonstrating understanding of my needs, and working with me to find a beneficial solution for both parties. Because of her efforts to build trust, my company was willing to consider her proposal, leading to a mutually beneficial outcome.

COMMUNICATION STYLES

Communication styles vary from culture to culture, and understanding these differences is necessary to communicating effectively with people from other cultures.

High-Context vs. Low-Context Communication

The concept of high-context and low-context communication, eloquently articulated by anthropologist Edward T. Hall, provides a valuable framework for understanding the nuanced ways in which cultures communicate. Mr. Hall said:

> *In high-context communication, most of the information is either in the physical context or internalized in the person, while in low-context communication, the mass of information is vested in the explicit code.*

In cultures that use high-context communication, the emphasis lies not solely on the explicit words spoken but also on the intricate tapestry of unspoken cues, shared history, and cultural nuances. Meaning is often derived from the context of the interaction itself, including factors such as relationships, social standing, and nonverbal cues like body language and tone of voice.

In contrast, cultures that use low-context communication place greater emphasis on explicit verbal communication. Messages are typically direct and unambiguous, with little reliance on implied meanings or shared understandings. Clear and concise language is paramount, and information is often conveyed through written documents, formal presentations, and explicit agreements.

Understanding these fundamental differences is crucial for navigating intercultural interactions with grace and sensitivity. By recognizing the varying degrees to which context influences communication, we can avoid misinterpretations, build stronger relationships, and foster more effective collaborations across cultures.

In addition, the concept of high-context and low-context communication extends beyond cultural interactions to influence the dynamics within organizations. For instance, creative fields, such as advertising and design, often thrive in a more high-context environment where ideas are exchanged through implicit cues, brainstorming sessions, and a shared understanding of the creative vision.

In contrast, fields like engineering and software development, where precision and clarity are paramount, may benefit from a low-context approach with clearly defined instructions, detailed documentation, and explicit communication protocols. Recognizing these inherent differences in communication styles within different departments and roles is crucial for effective collaboration and achieving organizational goals.

It's important to note that categorizing entire countries as definitively "high–context" or "low–context" can be overly simplistic. Communication styles within a single country vary significantly depending on factors such as region, social class, and individual personality. However, here is an overview based on general cultural tendencies.

High–Context Cultures:

- **Africa:** many countries, such as Ghana, Kenya, and Nigeria
- **Asia:** China, India, Indonesia, Japan, Korea, Malaysia, the Philippines, Thailand, and Vietnam
- **Latin America:** Argentina, Brazil, Colombia, and Mexico
- **Middle East:** Arab countries (Egypt, Saudi Arabia, and the United Arab Emirates—UAE), Iran, and Turkey

Low–Context Cultures:

- **Australia** and **New Zealand**
- **Europe:** Denmark, Germany, the Netherlands, Norway, Sweden, and Switzerland
- **North America:** Canada and the United States

It's crucial to remember that these are general tendencies, and individual communication styles may vary significantly within any given culture. Also, communication styles within a culture may evolve over time due to globalization, technological advancements, and other factors.

It's important when working with people from another culture to seek to understand the communication styles favored by that culture. By being aware of the cultural differences in communication styles, you can avoid misunderstandings that often occur when leaders from different cultures have different expectations about communication. By understanding these differences, you can avoid misinterpreting each other's intentions.

Being aware of cultural differences in communication style also allows you to adapt your communication style to suit the cultural context. For example, in a culture that values indirect communication, you may need to be more patient and allow time for others to express their preferences.

LANGUAGE

As you work with people from other cultures, chances are many will speak a language foreign to you. Gaining even a basic knowledge of that language is beneficial and will help break down cultural barriers. Learning key phrases and cultural idioms will facilitate more meaningful interactions, demonstrate respect for their culture, build trust, and help you connect with people on a deeper level.

If you choose to invest even more time and energy, developing fluency in another language can significantly enhance your intercultural relationships, open doors to new opportunities, enhance your cultural competence, and enrich your personal and professional life.

Speaking Through an Interpreter

Even when individuals share a common language, cultural differences in communication styles, idioms, and nonverbal cues often lead to misunderstandings and misinterpretations. To bridge these linguistic and cultural gaps, it is crucial to employ skilled language translators who deeply understand the languages and cultures of both parties.

When communicating through an interpreter, it is essential to speak clearly and concisely, maintain eye contact with the interpreter, and use wording that addresses the person you are speaking to, not the interpreter. Additionally, using simple language, avoiding jargon, and incorporating visual aids will enhance comprehension and minimize misinterpretations.

Cultural Expressions

Many cultural expressions are difficult for non-native speakers to understand, but making an effort to understand them is essential to becoming fluent in a language. Here are a few types of common cultural expressions:

- **Idioms:** Idioms are expressions with a symbolic meaning that differs from the words' literal meaning. For example, the English idiom "break a leg" means "good luck," but this expression would confuse someone who does not know the idiom.
- **Slang:** Slang is informal language used by a particular group. Slang vocabulary varies significantly across regions and cultures.
- **Regional dialects:** Regional dialects are language variations in different geographic areas. These dialects may have different pronunciation and grammar in addition to a different vocabulary.
- **Sarcasm:** Sarcasm involves stating the opposite of what you really mean, often in an effort to be humorous. But the humor is often misunderstood by native and non-native speakers alike. A person on the receiving end of sarcasm might end up feeling like the speaker is tricking them or laughing at their expense.

BUSINESS ETIQUETTE FOR SUCCESSFUL COMMUNICATION

There are also many cultural nuances specific to business etiquette. Here are a few examples.

Small Talk and Relationship Building

Cultural differences regarding relationship building can significantly impact the dynamics of meetings and negotiations. As mentioned earlier, in some cultures, building personal relationships is a crucial precursor to conducting business. Small talk and social interactions may be essential to establishing trust and rapport. In contrast, in other cultures, business is conducted more directly and efficiently, with a focus on the task at hand.

For example, in many Western cultures, meetings are often scheduled well in advance, and participants are expected to arrive on time and be prepared to discuss business. In contrast, in some Eastern cultures, relationships may be more important than punctuality, and meetings may be more flexible and less structured.

Hierarchy and Authority

The perception and significance of hierarchy and authority vary across cultures. In some cultures, hierarchical relationships are highly valued and decision-making authority is concentrated in the hands of senior leaders. In these cultures, it is important to show respect to superiors and follow established protocols.

For example, in Japan, it is important to address individuals by their titles and be deferential to superiors. In other cultures, a more egalitarian approach is preferred, with decisions made through consensus or democratic processes. Understanding these cultural differences is essential for effective cross-cultural collaboration.

Gift-Giving

Gift-giving in a business setting is a common practice in many cultures, but the significance and appropriateness of gift-giving varies widely. It is important to learn local customs and etiquette to avoid damaging relationships or hindering business deals. In some cultures, gifts are given to express gratitude and build relationships, while in others, gift-giving may be perceived as bribery.

In China, gift-giving is an important part of business culture, and it is customary to exchange gifts during negotiations. However, it is important to choose gifts carefully and avoid giving gifts that are too expensive or extravagant.

In most countries, doing business with government officials is a sensitive task, and gift-giving to government officials is generally frowned upon. Even hosting a meal with government officials may be problematic, with some countries setting limits on how much can be spent on such meals.

Time Management

Cultural differences can affect how time is perceived and valued. In some cultures, time is seen as a linear resource that can be measured and managed, while in others, time is seen as more cyclical and flexible. Some cultures have a long-term orientation, while others have a short-term orientation.

Deadlines and Punctuality

In some cultures, deadlines are treated as flexible guidelines, while in others, they are strictly adhered to. For instance, in many Western cultures, like in the USA, deadlines are often considered firm commitments, and punctuality is highly valued. The deadline is the end of the race. What's after the deadline? Maybe another phase, but not the same deadline.

In contrast, in some Eastern cultures, like in Nigeria, people may have a more relaxed approach to time. They prioritize relationships and long-term goals over strict adherence to deadlines. Deadlines are seen as more of a checkpoint. All members regroup and set a new deadline.

Also, in some cultures where they view time as scarce, a project finished just before the deadline is considered late. Singapore is one place where projects are expected to be completed well before the deadline.

It is essential to consider these cultural nuances when working with individuals from different backgrounds. When setting deadlines, it's important to be clear about expectations and allow for flexibility, especially when working with cultures that have a more relaxed approach to time. Also, effective communication and regular check-ins help ensure that projects stay on track and deadlines are met.

A Note about Negotiating

In today's interconnected world, business deals are often negotiated between organizations from different cultural backgrounds. Successful negotiation in international contexts requires a deep understanding of cultural nuances; effective communication; and a willingness to consider the needs and desires of all parties, adapt to various styles and approaches, find common ground, and compromise. As you negotiate, aim to find a win-win outcome that satisfies all parties' needs and interests. As you are genuinely concerned not only about how the results will benefit you and your organization but how they will benefit those you are negotiating with, you will develop trust and find more innovative solutions.

Thoroughly prepare for your negotiations by researching the other party's culture, business practices, and objectives. This will help you anticipate potential challenges and opportunities as you communicate with the other party.

Be flexible and adaptable to different negotiation styles and approaches. Be willing to adjust your strategy as needed to accommodate the other party's cultural preferences.

Finally, consider using cultural intermediaries to facilitate communication and bridge cultural gaps. Cultural intermediaries provide insights into cultural differences and help to navigate negotiations more effectively.

NONVERBAL COMMUNICATION—CULTURAL DIFFERENCES IN BODY LANGUAGE

It is easy to assume that all people around the world will understand your body language (facial expressions, gestures, proxemics—use of space) and other nonverbal communication—to assume that body language meaning is universal. However, there are significant differences in the use and interpretation of nonverbal communication that must be learned in order to avoid misunderstandings during cross-cultural interactions.

Eye Contact

In Western cultures (e.g., in North America and Northern Europe), direct eye contact is generally seen as a sign of respect, honesty, and engagement. In East Asian cultures (e.g., in Japan and Korea), prolonged eye contact may be considered rude or aggressive. Maintaining moderate eye contact is generally preferred. Those in some African cultures (e.g., in many West African cultures) consider direct eye contact, especially with elders or people of higher status, to be disrespectful.

Gestures

In Western cultures (e.g., in North America), the thumbs-up gesture is generally considered to be a positive sign. Pointing with the index finger is acceptable and common. In Middle Eastern cultures (e.g., in some Arab countries), the thumbs-up gesture and pointing with a single finger may be considered offensive. In India, generally, the thumbs-up gesture is positive. Pointing with the index finger is considered rude, so instead, people often point with their chin or use their whole hand.

Personal Space Preferences

In Western cultures (e.g., in North America and Northern Europe), personal space is highly valued—people generally prefer to maintain a larger personal space bubble and may feel uncomfortable if someone invades that bubble. In Latin American cultures (e.g., in Brazil and Mexico), physical contact and closer proximity are common and accepted. In Middle Eastern cultures (e.g., in some Arab countries), standing close to someone can be a sign of respect and friendship.

By being mindful of personal space preferences and adapting to local customs, you'll avoid misunderstandings and build stronger relationships with people from diverse backgrounds.

Facial Expressions

Reading faces is a universal art that is practiced every day. Ages ago in

China they even developed a method of face reading called *mianxiang*. The doctors and scientists of the educated and privileged class noted that body build and facial features profoundly influenced people's lives, from health and longevity to the degree of economic and social success they achieved. When we see other people's facial expressions, whether they reveal fear, anger, happiness, or other moods, we respond. Understanding how other cultures may interpret our facial expressions helps us avoid miscommunication.

Smiling

In many Western cultures, a smile is often interpreted as a sign of friendliness and approachability. However, in some East Asian cultures, a constant smile may be perceived as insincere or superficial.

Head Nodding

In many Western cultures, a nod typically signifies agreement or understanding. However, in some parts of the Middle East and South Asia, a slight nod can indicate disagreement or disapproval.

CASE STUDY: CROSS-CULTURAL COMMUNICATION

Early in my career as an executive, I (Bryan) was thrilled about a new assignment in Japan. I admired Japanese culture and was eager to experience the country firsthand. However, I soon discovered my enthusiasm alone was insufficient preparation to navigate the cultural nuances of doing business in Japan.

During my crucial first meeting with a potential Japanese client, eager to show interest and engagement, I maintained frequent eye contact and leaned forward toward my Japanese counterpart, not realizing that in Japanese culture, direct eye contact and physical closeness are often perceived as aggressive or confrontational. My lack of knowledge at that time about this cultural difference strained the relationship—I later learned the Japanese client had felt uncomfortable and found my behavior off-putting.

The meeting continued, but the initial misunderstanding created a barrier to effective communication. My direct style clashed with the more subtle and indirect communication style preferred by Japanese businesspeople. The Japanese client hesitated to express disagreement or ask for clarification, fearing it might be disrespectful.

As a result of the lack of cultural sensitivity, the meeting became increasingly tense and unproductive. I didn't understand why the Japanese client seemed so hesitant and withdrawn. The client, in turn, was frustrated by my perceived lack of sensitivity to Japanese cultural norms.

After the meeting, one of my colleagues helped me realize that my assumptions about Japanese culture had been inaccurate and I needed to adapt my communication style to be more culturally appropriate.

In an effort to understand how to better communicate with Japanese clients in the future, I sought advice from colleagues and mentors who had experience doing business in Japan. They explained the cultural significance of indirect communication and the importance of building relationships before discussing business matters. I also learned about "saving face," which is crucial in Japan and some other Asian cultures. It is essential to avoid embarrassing a person, or causing them to lose face, in front of others, as this can damage relationships.

With this new understanding, during my second meeting with the

Japanese client, I adapted my approach. I tried to build rapport and trust before discussing business matters. And I was patient, giving the client ample time to respond to my questions. I was more understanding as the client expressed themselves in their preferred way. I also avoided frequent direct eye contact and spoke with a softer voice. The meeting was a much more positive experience for both the client and me. The client felt more comfortable and respected, and the communication was more open and productive.

This experience taught me a valuable lesson about the importance of cultural awareness and sensitivity in international business. It also highlighted the need for open-mindedness and a willingness to learn from others. By understanding and respecting cultural differences, I overcame the initial misunderstanding and established a successful business relationship.

KEY TAKEAWAYS

Effective cross-cultural communication is essential for success in a globalized world. Understanding nonverbal cues, language barriers, and cultural nuances improves communication and helps build stronger relationships with people from different backgrounds.

Reflect on your organization's cross-cultural communication understanding. What are your strengths and weaknesses? How can you improve your organization's cross-cultural communication?

Chapter 5

INTERCULTURAL CONFLICT RESOLUTION

Conflicts can arise in any context, but they are particularly challenging to address when they involve people from different cultural backgrounds. This chapter explores the reasons for many intercultural conflicts, how to avoid them, and strategies for effectively resolving them.

> *Note: Throughout this chapter, the classifications ascribed to various countries are generalizations, and there may be variations within countries. Cultural dimensions also change over time due to various factors such as globalization and modernization.*

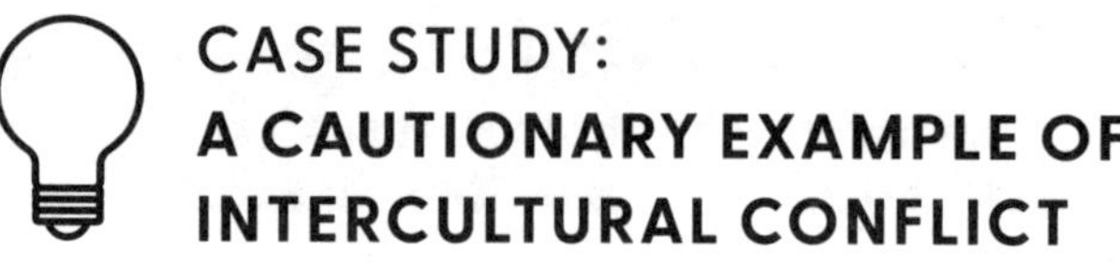

CASE STUDY: A CAUTIONARY EXAMPLE OF INTERCULTURAL CONFLICT

A senior leader of an international Fortune 100 consumer goods company, new to South Korea, learned a lesson the hard way when he unilaterally changed job titles across his entire company. In South Korea, job titles hold significant weight, often reflecting a person's social status, education, and professional accomplishments. Unlike in Western cultures, job titles are more hierarchical, resembling military ranks. This emphasis on hierarchy is deeply ingrained in Korean culture and influences how individuals are perceived and treated.

Koreans frequently use dual titles, combining a Korean seniority rank with an English functional title. This practice is widespread in business settings where it helps to convey both the individual's position within the organization and their expertise. For instance, as a sign of respect, a restaurant owner might be addressed as "President" in English and "Sajang" in Korean.

The business leader who changed his employees' job titles failed to recognize this South Korean custom, and his actions caused widespread employee resentment and confusion, decreasing morale and productivity. The leader ultimately realized the importance of consulting with employees and considering cultural implications when making decisions for his international company. He began consulting with the human resources director on all job title issues and ended up restoring most employees' job titles.

COMMON CAUSES OF INTERCULTURAL CONFLICT

Here are some of the common causes of intercultural conflict:

- misunderstandings because of differences in communication styles, cultural norms, values, beliefs, expectations, language, and so on
- ethnocentrism, or the belief that one's culture is superior to others
- racism or nationalism—discriminatory attitudes and behaviors based on race, ethnicity, or nationality
- power imbalances—whether because of economic disparities, political influence, or cultural differences—when one group feels they have more control or influence over the situation (example: when a person does business with someone from a country that is less powerful than their own)

These root causes of intercultural conflict underscore the critical importance of understanding and appreciating the diverse perspectives and values that shape human societies. By cultivating a deeper understanding of different cultures, we can bridge these divides, foster mutual respect, avoid conflicts, and create a more harmonious and interconnected world.

MODELS FOR UNDERSTANDING DIFFERENCES IN CULTURAL VALUES

Cultivating a deeper understanding of cultural differences is paramount in navigating the intricate tapestry of human interaction and fostering harmonious relationships across diverse societies. The following models offer valuable frameworks for exploring and comprehending the nuanced variations that exist among cultures.

Hofstede's Cultural Dimensions Model

Geert Hofstede introduced a model identifying various dimensions in which cultures vary: individualism vs. collectivism, power distance, uncertainty avoidance, and masculinity vs. femininity.

Individualism vs. Collectivism

Individualistic cultures prioritize individual needs and goals, while collectivist cultures emphasize group harmony and loyalty. In individualistic cultures, people may be more likely to speak their minds and assert their own opinions. In contrast, in collectivist cultures, people may be more likely to prioritize the group's needs over their own.

People from individualistic cultures prioritize individual needs and goals. They prioritize individuality, personal achievement, privacy, self-reliance, and independence. In contrast, those from collectivist cultures prioritize group harmony and loyalty. They value cohesion, duty, pursuing goals as a group, and interdependence. They are more about "us" and "we" than "I" or "me."

Generally Considered Individualistic Cultures:

- **Australia** and **New Zealand**
- **Europe:** France, Germany, the Netherlands, Switzerland, and the United Kingdom
- **North America:** Canada and the United States
- **South Africa**

Generally Considered Collectivist Cultures:

- **Africa:** many countries, including Ghana, Kenya, and Nigeria
- **Asia:** China, India, Indonesia, Japan, Korea, Malaysia, the Philippines, Thailand, and Vietnam
- **Latin America:** Argentina, Brazil, Colombia, and Mexico
- **Middle East:** Arab countries (Egypt, Saudi Arabia, and the UAE), Iran, and Turkey

Power Distance

Power distance refers to how people accept inequality in power and authority. In high–power distance cultures, there is a greater emphasis on hierarchy and respect for authority figures. In low–power distance cultures, there is a greater emphasis on equality and participation.

High–Power Distance Cultures:

- **Africa:** many countries, including Ghana, Kenya, and Nigeria
- **Asia:** China, India, Indonesia, Japan, Korea, Malaysia, the Philippines, Singapore, Taiwan, and Thailand
- **Latin America:** Brazil, Colombia, Mexico, and Venezuela
- **Middle East:** Egypt, Iran, Kuwait, Saudi Arabia, and the UAE

Low–Power Distance Cultures:

- **Australia** and **New Zealand**
- **Europe:** Austria, Denmark, Finland, Germany, the Netherlands, Norway, Sweden, and Switzerland
- **Israel**
- **North America:** Canada and the United States

Uncertainty Avoidance

Uncertainty avoidance is the degree to which people feel uncomfortable with uncertainty and ambiguity. In high–uncertainty avoidance cultures, there is a greater emphasis on rules, regulations, and planning. In low–uncertainty avoidance cultures, people are more comfortable with risk and ambiguity.

High–Uncertainty Avoidance Cultures:

- **Asia:** China, Japan, South Korea, and Taiwan
- **Europe:** Belgium, France, Germany, Greece, Italy, Portugal, and Spain
- **Latin America:** Argentina, Chile, and Mexico

Low–Uncertainty Avoidance Cultures:

- **Australia** and **New Zealand**
- **Europe:** Denmark, Finland, Norway, Sweden, and the United Kingdom
- **North America:** Canada and the United States
- **Singapore**

Masculinity vs. Femininity

Masculinity and femininity refer to the degree to which societal roles are traditionally masculine or feminine. In masculine cultures, there is a greater emphasis on assertiveness, competition, and achievement. In feminine cultures, there is a greater emphasis on cooperation, caring, and quality of life.

Masculine Cultures:

- **Asia:** China, Hong Kong, Japan, South Korea, and Taiwan
- **Europe:** Austria, Germany, Switzerland, and the United Kingdom

- **Latin America:** Mexico
- **North America:** the United States
- **West Africa**

Feminine Cultures:

- **Africa:** Angola, Burkina Faso, Cameroon, East Africa, Ghana, Nigeria, and Sierra Leone
- **Costa Rica**
- **Europe:** Denmark, Finland, France, Italy, the Netherlands, Norway, Spain, and Sweden

The Lewis Model of Cultural Types

Richard Lewis created another model for understanding cultural differences. He concluded that cultures can be divided into three types: linear-active, multi-active, and reactive.

Linear-Active

People from linear-active cultures are task-oriented, organized, logical, and direct, and they prefer to get things done one task at a time. This type includes the English-speaking world, Northern Europe, and Scandinavia.

Multi-Active

People from multi-active cultures are emotional, expressive, and people-oriented. They see family, feelings, and relationships as more important than following an agenda. This type includes Arab and other cultures in the Middle East, Central America, India, Mediterranean countries, Pakistan, Russia, most Slavic countries, South America, Southern Europe, and sub-Saharan Africa.

Reactive

People from reactive cultures are polite, attentive listeners who are less likely to initiate action or discussion. They react and form their own opinions. These cultures are relationship-oriented, respectful, and indirect. This type includes all major countries in Asia except the Indian sub-continent.

As we use these models to better understand cultural differences, we can better avoid and resolve conflicts.

CULTURAL APPROACHES TO AVOIDING CONFLICT

Many intercultural problems can be avoided as leaders are aware of the following five cultural approaches.

First, a *cultural dominance-imposed approach.* A culture dominance-imposed approach is when someone from one culture imposes its values and ways of behaving on someone from a subordinate culture. For example, sometimes Koreans will insist to non-Koreans who are in Korea that they should do things the Korean way. It is a Roman telling a non-Roman, "When in Rome, do as the Romans do."

When on the receiving end of a cultural dominance-imposed approach, it may be advisable to negotiate or submit, depending on the circumstances. One example of when it would be advisable to submit by adhering to the customs of the host culture is when dealing with sensitive issues such as gift-giving.

Individuals demonstrate cultural sensitivity and build stronger relationships by respecting local customs and traditions when they visit or do business in another country. However, some companies have strict ethical and business practices that they enforce globally, knowingly ignoring local customs and insisting on their global best practices guidelines. Companies must carefully consider if such an approach is necessary in each country they do business with.

A second effective approach to avoiding intercultural conflict is *leveraging cultural differences*. In 2023, our global executive search partner, Kestria, successfully leveraged cultural differences at their global meetings in Tokyo. The team-building activity selected was learning how to play samurai drums together harmoniously. Also, we had an evening boat ride that included karaoke singing and eating traditional Japanese sashimi. By adapting team-building activities to local customs and surroundings, and in other ways leveraging cultural differences, companies can create a more inclusive and enjoyable experience for employees from diverse cultural backgrounds.

Thirdly, a *cultural compromise* may be advisable when two or more cultures share similar values and practices. One way for an international company to make a cultural compromise is to honor holidays in each country where they do business based on the traditions of each country. For example, a Norwegian client of ours that has offices in Asia handles the Lunar New Year holiday differently in different locations. While they don't celebrate the holiday in the Norwegian headquarters, in China they give employees an entire week off, as is customary there, and in Korea, they follow local customs by giving employees three days off and a set financial gift or equivalent fruit or meat gift box.

Making cultural compromises may be more challenging when cultural differences are more pronounced. It is essential to carefully assess the similarities and differences between cultures to determine the feasibility of compromise as a solution.

Finally, *cultural accommodation* involves adapting to and integrating with a different culture by adopting its beliefs, values, and practices in an effort to avoid or solve problems.

In some cases, adopting the local culture's solutions may be the most appropriate course of action. However, it is vital to consider the specific context and the relative strengths of the cultures involved. It is also essential to evaluate the potential benefits and drawbacks of cultural accommodation and to ensure that it does not compromise the integrity of one's own cultural identity.

Cultural accommodation came into play when a multinational company decided to establish a subsidiary in Japan. In order to successfully operate in this new market, the company's leaders implemented several strategies to adapt to Japanese business practices:

- **Respect for hierarchy:** The company understands the importance of hierarchical relationships in Japanese culture. It ensures that decisions are made through formal channels and that superiors are treated with appropriate respect.
- **Emphasis on relationships:** The company invests time in building strong relationships with Japanese business partners and clients. This involves engaging in social activities, exchanging gifts, and participating in traditional cultural events.
- **Subtle communication:** The company recognizes that Japanese communication styles are often more indirect and nuanced than those of Western cultures. Therefore, they adapt their communication style to be more polite and respectful and less confrontational.
- **Patience and perseverance:** The company understands that building trust and establishing long-term relationships takes time. Therefore, it is patient and persistent in its approach to business dealings.

By accommodating Japanese cultural norms and practices, the company builds strong relationships, builds trust, and achieves business success in the Japanese market. However, the company is careful to balance cultural accommodation with maintaining the company's core values and business principles.

STRATEGIES FOR RESOLVING INTERCULTURAL CONFLICT

Although sensitivity and a culturally aware approach help prevent many potential intercultural conflicts, conflicts will inevitably arise in a global company. But as these conflicts are handled appropriately, companies will overcome challenges and be stronger for them. Here are some helpful strategies for resolving intercultural conflicts:

- **Employ active listening:** Really listening to what the other party says will help you better understand and address their perspective in order to come to a solution.
- **Be empathetic:** Try to see things from the other person's point of view and have genuine concern for their situation.
- **Be open-minded:** Be open to different viewpoints and avoid making assumptions.
- **Be respectful:** Treat others with respect, regardless of their cultural background.
- **Be patient:** Be patient and understanding, especially when dealing with cultural differences.
- **Seek cultural training:** Cultural training will help you understand and navigate cultural differences between you and your colleagues. And with greater understanding, resolving conflicts will be easier.

- **Employ a third-party mediator:** If you cannot resolve a conflict alone, consider involving a neutral third party.

KEY TAKEAWAYS

Intercultural conflict is a complex issue that requires careful attention and understanding. It can arise from differences in values, beliefs, communication styles, and expectations. To resolve intercultural conflicts effectively, it is essential to develop a global mindset and approach cultural differences with understanding, practice active listening and empathy, and be open-minded and respectful.

Reflect on intercultural conflicts your organization has had in the past. How could they have been avoided? Were they handled effectively?

Are there practices that need to be implemented or training that needs to be provided in your organization to better avoid intercultural conflicts in the future?

Reflect on the strengths and weaknesses of your organization's intercultural conflict resolution practices. How can you improve your organization's approach to intercultural conflict resolution?

Chapter 6

NAVIGATING IN-GROUP AND OUT-GROUP DYNAMICS

The concept of in-groups and out-groups is fundamental to human social behavior, shaping interactions across cultures. In many societies, particularly those with strong collectivist values, the distinction between in-groups and out-groups significantly influences social relationships, expectations, and behaviors, including in a business environment. Learning how to navigate in-group and out-group dynamics is essential for intercultural business success.

IN-GROUPS AND OUT-GROUPS IN VARIOUS CULTURES

African Cultures

Tribal affiliations and kinship networks often serve as the cornerstone of in-group identity in African cultures. Shared ancestry and geographic origin play a significant role in defining who belongs and who remains an outsider. In-group affiliations provide a strong sense of belonging and support, offering a safety net in times of need and fostering a deep sense of community.

Within these intricate networks, individuals find solace, support, and a shared sense of purpose. However, this strong sense of in-group identity may also contribute to conflicts within an in-group, particularly when groups are competing for resources. Historical grievances, past conflicts, and perceived threats to in-group interests sometimes exacerbate tensions and perpetuate cycles of mistrust and animosity.

East Asian Cultures

In East Asian cultures, such as Korean, Japanese, and Chinese, the concept of in-groups and out-groups is deeply ingrained, shaping daily social interactions. In-groups (often referred to as *guanxi* in China) are characterized by strong bonds of loyalty, trust, and mutual obligation and often revolve around family, close friends, colleagues, and individuals who share a common history, language, or social status. These groups prioritize collective harmony and the group's well-being over individual needs. Within in-groups, social interactions are typically characterized by warmth, familiarity, and a high degree of trust.

Conversely, interactions with out-groups tend to be more formal, distant, and characterized by a greater degree of caution and reserve.

The emphasis on in-group harmony sometimes leads to a preference for cooperation and consensus within the in-group, disregarding dissent, sometimes at the expense of individual expression.

South Asian Cultures

In countries like India and Pakistan, caste and religious affiliations exert a profound influence on social structures and individual identities, shaping the intricate web of in-group/out-group dynamics. While the caste system, a complex social hierarchy, was officially abolished many decades ago, it still plays a significant role in determining social status, access to resources, and even occupational opportunities. Individuals within a particular caste often experience a strong sense of belonging and shared identity, fostering a deep sense of loyalty and mutual support amongst their members.

Similarly, religious affiliation significantly influences in-group/out-group dynamics in South Asian cultures. Individuals may prioritize the interests and well-being of their own religious community, leading to potential conflicts or tensions with other religious groups.

This strong in-group affiliation sometimes contributes to social stratification and discrimination. Intercaste marriages, for instance, may face social disapproval or even ostracism.

Latin American Cultures

Latin American cultures deeply value family, with strong bonds extending beyond immediate family to encompass extended kin, godparents, and close friends. Intricate networks of familial and social relationships form the bedrock of Latin American societies, creating a powerful sense of belonging and shared identity. Family obligations often take precedence, influencing decisions related to work, leisure, and social interactions. This emphasis on family fosters a strong sense of loyalty, support, and collective responsibility within the in-group.

However, this strong sense of familial obligation presents challenges in certain contexts. For instance, prioritizing family needs may sometimes impact work commitments, leading to potential conflicts between professional and personal responsibilities. Furthermore, the emphasis on personal relationships and trust within the in-group sometimes leads to favoritism or nepotism in professional settings.

Middle Eastern Cultures

In many Middle Eastern cultures, family and religious and tribal affiliations form the cornerstone of social identity, weaving a complex tapestry of interconnected relationships. Strong ties of loyalty, kinship, and shared history bind individuals together within in-groups, fostering a deep sense of belonging and mutual support. These in-groups often extend beyond immediate family to encompass extended kin, clan members, and even broader tribal affiliations.

This intricate web of social connections shapes individual behavior and social interactions. Loyalty to the in-group is paramount, often taking precedence over personal interests. This strong sense of collective identity fosters a deep understanding of responsibility toward fellow in-group members, with obligations to assist and support one another in need. However, this emphasis on in-group loyalty sometimes leads to distrust and suspicion of out-groups, potentially contributing to intergroup tensions and conflicts.

It's crucial to recognize that for all of these cultures, these are just generalizations, and individual experiences and cultural nuances may vary significantly within any given society.

STRATEGIES FOR NAVIGATING IN-GROUP AND OUT-GROUP DYNAMICS

Understanding the dynamics and working within the framework of in-groups and out-groups is paramount for navigating the complexities of intercultural business interactions. While we may initially be perceived as outsiders or members of the out-group in a foreign culture, there are avenues to bridge these divides and foster a sense of belonging.

Find Common Ground

One strategy for navigating in-group/out-group dynamics is finding common ground. For instance, shared passions, interests, and affiliations can be powerful bridges, transcending cultural boundaries. A shared love for music, sports, or a particular hobby can quickly transform strangers into newfound friends, forging unexpected connections across cultural lines.

In addition, shared values and beliefs can serve as powerful unifying forces. Religious affiliation, for instance, can provide a sense of shared purpose and community, transcending cultural differences. When individuals from different cultural backgrounds come together to worship, participate in religious ceremonies, or engage in community service activities, they may quickly find common ground and develop strong bonds of solidarity.

Similarly, professional affiliations can foster a sense of in-group belonging. Individuals working in the same industry, particularly in multinational corporations, often develop strong professional networks, regardless of their cultural backgrounds. Shared professional goals, challenges, and experiences can create a sense of camaraderie and shared purpose, transcending cultural differences and fostering collaboration.

Build Strong Relationships

When living internationally, investing time in building strong relationships with individuals from the host culture will go a long way in helping you be accepted as a member of the in-group. Seek opportunities for genuine connection, such as sharing meals, attending cultural events, or engaging in shared hobbies. For example, a foreign businessperson might join a local golf or other club to build relationships with potential clients and partners.

CASE STUDY: A US–JAPANESE DEAL

A US company eager to expand its operations in the Japanese market entered into negotiations with a prominent Japanese corporation. The American negotiators, accustomed to a direct and task-oriented approach, were surprised by their Japanese counterparts' seemingly indirect and relationship-focused approach. There were in-group/out-group dynamics at play, and cultural differences initially created misunderstandings and challenges in the negotiation process.

The American negotiators expected the Japanese to focus more on the deal. They were surprised when the Japanese negotiators seemed more interested in discussing personal interests, hobbies, and shared experiences. This initial focus on relationship building was unfamiliar to the Americans, who were accustomed to a more transactional approach.

However, as the negotiations progressed, the American negotiators began to understand the cultural significance of relationship building in Japan. In Japanese culture, business deals are often seen as an extension of personal relationships rather than purely transactional agreements.

The American negotiators realized they needed to adapt their approach to be more relationship oriented and make efforts to help themselves be perceived as members of the Japanese negotiators' in-group rather than as outsiders. They spent more time getting to know their Japanese counterparts personally, discussing shared interests, and building trust. They also avoided being too direct or pushy, allowing the Japanese negotiators to lead the conversations. This ultimately led to a successful negotiation and a mutually beneficial agreement.

Be Respectful of Communication Norms

As discussed in chapter 4, communication norms, both verbal and nonverbal, vary significantly across cultures. Making an effort to understand these cultural differences is essential for avoiding misunderstandings and building in-group relationships with people from diverse backgrounds.

Seek Mentorship

Find a mentor who can guide you through understanding cultural nuances and help you build relationships with in-group members. This could be a colleague, friend, or professional mentor. And they could be either a local or a foreigner who has successfully learned to navigate in-group dynamics in the culture you are interacting with. A mentor can provide valuable insights into local customs, business practices, and social etiquette.

Practice Patience and Perseverance

Building strong relationships with people from different cultures takes effort. It takes time to develop trust and rapport, especially when navigating cultural differences. Be patient and persistent when connecting with others and avoid rushing through the process. By investing time and energy in building relationships, you will create lasting connections that transcend cultural boundaries and increase your odds of being accepted as a member of the in-group.

Learn the Language

Immerse yourself in the local language to deepen your understanding of the society. Language proficiency will significantly enhance your ability to become part of an in-group in another country.

Respect Cultural Norms and Customs

Learning local customs, traditions, and etiquette will help you demonstrate respect, build trust, and eventually be accepted in the in-group. Avoid behaviors that may be considered offensive or disrespectful. For instance, in many Asian cultures, refusing a host's gift or drink is considered impolite. If one does not show proper respect for the culture, they will be considered a member of the out-group.

Be Humble and Seek Feedback

Acknowledge your cultural limitations and be open to learning from others. Avoid arrogance and ethnocentrism. Avoid making assumptions or imposing your expectations of cultural norms on others.

Actively seek feedback from local colleagues and friends. Invite them to help you identify areas where you need to improve in your communication, behavior, and understanding of their culture. Be open to their honest and constructive criticism, viewing it as an invaluable opportunity for growth and learning. Doing so will gradually bridge the gap between yourself and the in-group.

While all of these strategies will be helpful in navigating in-group/out-group dynamics, it is crucial to acknowledge that these dynamics are complex and nuanced. Power imbalances, perceived threats, and existing social hierarchies sometimes impede the process of inclusion. You will achieve the greatest success as you approach intercultural interactions with humility, respect, and a genuine desire to understand and appreciate the perspectives of others.

KEY TAKEAWAYS

In-groups and out-groups are a fundamental aspect of human society, profoundly influencing our interactions and relationships, particularly in the global business arena. In many societies, individuals gravitate toward those they perceive as "like them," forming strong bonds within these in-groups.

These groups, whether based on family, ethnicity, religion, shared interests, or professional affiliations, provide a sense of belonging, security, and support.

Recognizing and navigating these intricate social structures is crucial for successful business operations in the globalized world. While we may initially be perceived as outsiders within a new market or business environment, there are avenues to bridge these divides and foster a sense of belonging within the in-group. By actively seeking common ground, demonstrating genuine curiosity and respect for local customs and traditions, and building relationships based on trust and mutual understanding, you will be more likely to become a valued member of the in-group and enable your organization to cultivate strong partnerships, enhance their market presence, and achieve long-term success in diverse cultural contexts.

Reflect on your organization's understanding of in-groups and out-groups. What are your strengths and weaknesses? How can you help your employees from one office be included in the in-group with employees at other offices? How can you help your employees be included in the in-group with clients and other stakeholders? In what other ways can you improve your organization's in-group/out-group dynamics in the countries where you do business?

Chapter 7

ATTRACTING, RETAINING, AND CULTIVATING TALENT

The business world is undergoing unprecedented changes. Technological advancements, demographic shifts, and evolving customer demands are reshaping the landscape for organizations of all sizes. In today's interconnected world, organizations must have access to a diverse and skilled workforce to remain competitive.

Effective talent management for a global organization involves attracting and retaining top talent as well as nurturing individuals from various cultural backgrounds to prepare them to be successful international leaders.

In this chapter, we'll explore key trends shaping the business world and discuss the implications for executive search and retaining and cultivating future talent. We'll also share insights we've gained through leading McKinney Consulting, our executive search firm, which has served Fortune 100 companies for almost twenty-five years, on how to adapt your approach to talent acquisition and ensure you attract the best leaders for your organization's future.

CASE STUDY: ACCENTURE

Accenture, a multinational professional services giant, has successfully navigated the complexities of attracting, cultivating, and retaining a diverse global workforce. To foster a cohesive and productive work environment, Accenture has implemented several strategic initiatives.

One such initiative is comprehensive cultural training. By equipping employees with a deep understanding of different cultures, Accenture empowers them to communicate effectively, build strong relationships, and collaborate seamlessly with colleagues from various backgrounds.

In addition, Accenture cultivates a diverse and adaptable workforce by providing opportunities for cross-cultural assignments. The company's global mobility program enables employees to gain valuable international experience, fostering a sense of global citizenship and enhancing their career development.

Accenture also leverages cutting-edge virtual team tools to facilitate collaboration among geographically dispersed teams. These tools enable seamless communication, real-time collaboration, and knowledge sharing, regardless of location.

Finally, Accenture's global compensation and benefits strategy ensures fairness and equity across all regions. By offering competitive compensation packages and comprehensive benefits, the company attracts and retains top talent worldwide.

Through these strategic initiatives, Accenture has created a truly global workforce united by a common purpose and empowered to drive innovation and deliver exceptional results.

THE EVOLVING TALENT LANDSCAPE

In recent years, the talent pool landscape has significantly changed in many ways, including the following.

Skill Shortage

New technologies have created a significant demand for specialized skills in areas like automation, artificial intelligence (AI), and data analytics. At the same time, the talent pool for these skills is often limited, making it challenging to find qualified candidates.

Shifting Priorities

Today's workforce prioritizes work-life balance, opportunities for continuous learning, and purpose-driven professional pursuits. Staying abreast of the latest priorities and aligning your company culture and values with these priorities will be crucial for attracting top talent.

Remote Work

The increasing expectation in some cultures of being able to work remotely, along with the rise of remote work technologies, has blurred geographic boundaries, allowing companies to tap into a global talent pool. However, this change necessitates new strategies for team collaboration, performance management, and building a solid company culture.

ATTRACTING TOP TALENT

As the global talent landscape continues to evolve, organizations must adapt their recruitment strategies to attract and retain top talent. Organizations need to build a strong employer brand, utilize global recruitment channels, and demonstrate cultural sensitivity throughout the recruitment process. Leveraging employee referral programs may also be a powerful tool for attracting high-quality candidates.

Ultimately, attracting top talent hinges on creating a compelling employer value proposition. By fostering a positive work environment and prioritizing employee growth and development, organizations establish themselves as employers of choice in the global talent market.

Recommendations for You, the Hiring Manager

As a hiring manager, you're at the forefront of building your organization's leadership team. To navigate the changing landscape of talent acquisition, consider the following.

Define Your Needs Clearly

Clearly articulate your company's goals and the specific skills, experience, and cultural fit you desire in a candidate. A well-defined job description will help you attract the most qualified candidates and streamline the hiring process.

Embrace Technology

Leverage AI and data analytics to enhance your search process and identify qualified candidates. In recruiting, AI and other data analyzing tools can analyze resumes by quickly scanning and identifying key skills, experiences, and keywords. AI tools can search vast databases, looking beyond traditional job boards to find hidden talent on social media, in professional networks, and from other sources. They can also predict candidate success by analyzing past hiring data to identify patterns and predict which candidates are most likely to succeed in a role. And finally, AI tools can automate repetitive tasks. For example, they can schedule interviews and send reminders, freeing up recruiters to focus on more strategic work.

Create a Positive Candidate Experience

You can create positive and engaging experiences for candidates throughout the hiring process by providing accurate, useful information about your company and the role, making the process transparent, and promptly communicating with candidates throughout the process.

Focus on Future Skills

Consider global trends and your vision of your industry's future to identify candidates who possess the skills needed to thrive in your organization, not only now but for years to come. These skills may include critical thinking, problem-solving, creativity, and digital literacy. Look for leaders who adapt, are open to learning, and demonstrate a willingness to embrace change.

Continue Learning

Stay up to date on industry trends, emerging technologies, and best practices in talent acquisition. It's important to make informed decisions and stay ahead of the curve.

Partner with a Trusted Executive Search Firm

A skilled executive search firm will provide valuable expertise and resources to help you identify and attract top talent, even in challenging markets. Look for a firm with a proven track record in your industry and a deep understanding of the current talent landscape.

Here are some additional attributes to look for when selecting an executive search firm:

- **Global reach:** Partnering with an executive search firm that specializes in global talent acquisition will provide access to a wider pool of qualified candidates from diverse markets. These firms have the expertise to identify and attract highly skilled professionals with the necessary cultural competence and language skills needed to thrive in a globalized environment.
- **Deep industry expertise:** More than ever, your executive search partner needs a deep understanding of your specific industry and its challenges. Look for a firm with a proven track record of placing candidates in similar roles within your sector.
- **Data-driven approach:** A firm that has expanded beyond traditional search methods to leverage data analytics and AI will best be able to identify high-potential candidates who may not be actively searching for new opportunities.
- **Candidate experience:** Choose a firm that provides a positive experience not only for you but also for job candidates. Candidates expect executive search firms to be professional, considerate of their time, and transparent and honest in their communication.

In addition to finding the right talent, it's essential to create an environment where that talent can thrive—an environment that helps you retain top talent.

RETAINING TALENT

Retaining top global talent requires a multifaceted approach that goes beyond competitive salaries. While competitive compensation packages are essential, they are not enough to attract and retain the best employees in today's competitive global market.

For instance, it is crucial to foster an inclusive and supportive work environment that values diverse perspectives and respects individual differences. This includes creating a culture of open communication so that employees feel comfortable sharing their ideas and concerns without fear of judgment or reprisal.

Furthermore, cultivating a positive company culture that emphasizes employee well-being and work-life balance is paramount. This can be achieved through offering flexible work arrangements such as remote work options, flexible schedules, and generous parental leave policies.

Investing in employee development is another key factor. Providing opportunities for skill enhancement, mentorship programs, and career advancement not only benefits employees but also strengthens the organization as a whole.

Recognizing and rewarding employee contributions is also vital. Implementing a robust system of employee recognition can significantly boost morale, motivation, and loyalty.

This may include:

- **Publicly acknowledging achievements:** celebrating successes in team meetings, company newsletters, or social media platforms.
- **Offering tangible rewards:** providing bonuses, gift cards, or company-sponsored events to recognize outstanding performance.
- **Providing opportunities for growth:** recognizing high-performing employees with promotions, increased responsibilities, and leadership opportunities.

By implementing these strategies, organizations create a compelling employer value proposition that attracts and retains top global talent, fostering a high-performing and engaged workforce.

CULTIVATING FUTURE GLOBAL TALENT

Organizations should invest in global mobility programs—programs that send employees across international borders for work purposes, such as international transfers, rotations, cultural immersion experiences, mentorship programs, and other assignments—to equip their employees with the skills and knowledge to thrive in a globalized world. In addition, investing in cross-cultural training and leadership development initiatives will develop a pipeline of future global leaders.

To attract and retain current talent and develop future global leaders, IBM has implemented a comprehensive suite of training programs, including the following.

Cultural Training

IBM provides extensive cultural training programs to its employees, covering topics such as cross-cultural communication, intercultural sensitivity, and navigating cultural differences. These programs equip employees with the necessary skills to work effectively with colleagues from diverse backgrounds.

Language Training

The company offers language training programs to employees working in different regions, enabling them to communicate effectively with local clients and colleagues.

Global Mobility Programs

IBM provides opportunities for employees to gain international experience through global assignments, international projects, and cross-cultural exchanges. These programs foster a global mindset and enhance employees' intercultural competence.

International Leadership Program

This flagship program develops future leaders with a global perspective. The program focuses on developing critical leadership skills, such as cultural intelligence, cross-cultural communication, and global business acumen.

These initiatives not only help IBM attract and retain top talent from around the world but have also contributed to the company's success in the global marketplace by helping it be innovative, solve complex challenges, and better serve the needs of its global customer base. This commitment to maintaining a global mindset has positioned IBM as a leader in the technology industry and a model for other organizations seeking to build a truly global workforce.

KEY TAKEAWAYS

In today's interconnected world, attracting, retaining, and cultivating a diverse and globally minded workforce is paramount for organizational success. This chapter has explored the critical elements of effective global talent management and emphasized the importance of understanding and adapting to the evolving talent landscape.

We've emphasized the importance of demonstrating cultural sensitivity throughout the hiring process and fostering a positive work environment. And we've discussed the importance of providing competitive compensation and benefits, offering opportunities for professional development and growth, and prioritizing employee well-being.

By investing in your employees' growth, providing opportunities for international experience, and fostering a culture of continuous learning, organizations can cultivate a high-performing and globally minded workforce equipped to thrive in the ever-changing landscape of the twenty-first century.

Reflect on your organization's global talent management practices. What are your strengths and weaknesses? How can you improve your organization's ability to attract and manage a successful international workforce?

Chapter 8

NAVIGATING ETHICS IN A GLOBALIZED WORLD

In today's world, ethical considerations have become increasingly complex. They are no longer confined to individual actions but are deeply woven into the fabric of our global society. As businesses and individuals navigate the complexities of the international landscape, they inevitably encounter a range of moral dilemmas. The choices made in these situations have profound consequences, impacting not only personal reputations and relationships but also the success and sustainability of businesses and the well-being of entire communities.

As businesses and individuals operate globally, it is essential to consider ethical implications beyond those of your culture. Ethical decision-making requires a nuanced understanding of cultural differences, legal frameworks, and international norms.

FOSTERING AN ETHICAL CULTURE

As you seek to promote an ethical culture in your organization, vital ethical considerations include human rights, environmental sustainability, social responsibility, anti-corruption, data privacy and security, and acting with principle and sincerity.

Human Rights

Respecting human rights, including labor rights such as fair wages, safe working conditions, and freedom of association, is fundamental to ethical business practices. Companies should ensure their supply chains are free from exploitation and abuse.

Environmental Sustainability

Minimizing environmental impact and promoting sustainable practices are crucial for long-term business success and global well-being. Ethical companies recognize their responsibility to operate in an environmentally conscious manner and adopt eco-friendly practices such as reducing carbon emissions and conserving resources.

Social Responsibility

Companies should strive to contribute positively to the communities where they operate by supporting social and charitable causes. This may involve volunteering, donating to charities, and or implementing corporate social responsibility initiatives.

Anti-Corruption

Adhering to anti-corruption laws and regulations is essential to maintain ethical integrity. Companies should establish robust compliance programs and encourage employees to report any instances of corruption or bribery.

The following are important actions to take to discourage corruption in your organization:

- **Set the example:** Company leaders need to set a clear example of ethical behavior for employees to emulate. When leaders compromise ethical standards, employees might assume they have a pass to behave unethically as well.
- **Establish ethical guidelines and codes of conduct:** Develop comprehensive ethical guidelines and codes of conduct that outline your organization's values and expectations.
- **Implement ethics training programs:** Provide regular ethics training to employees to enhance their ethical awareness and decision-making skills.
- **Create a safe reporting environment:** Establish a confidential reporting mechanism to encourage employees to report unethical behavior without fear of retaliation.
- **Take swift and appropriate action:** Investigate misconduct allegations promptly and take appropriate disciplinary action against those violating ethical standards.

Data Privacy and Security

Protecting personal data and ensuring data privacy is paramount in today's digital age. Companies should implement strong data protection measures and comply with relevant data privacy laws and regulations.

Acting with Principle and Sincerity

Acting with principle and sincerity builds a foundation of trust and respect, fostering genuine relationships with colleagues, clients, and partners. Leaders must demonstrate consistency between their words and actions, upholding ethical standards even in the face of adversity.

When organizations foster a culture of integrity, they build trust with stakeholders, mitigate risks, and avoid roadblocks to success.

CULTURAL VALUES

Understanding and prioritizing our cultural values—the deeply ingrained principles that guide our beliefs and actions—is crucial for personal and professional fulfillment. By aligning your actions with your core values, you can make choices that give you a sense of purpose and meaning. For example, if personal growth is a high priority for you, you might prioritize learning and self-improvement opportunities. If family is a top value, you might prioritize spending quality time with loved ones and creating a strong family bond.

Cultural values form a hierarchical system that varies significantly across cultures. These hierarchies dictate how individuals prioritize values like honesty, loyalty, respect, and personal achievement, ultimately influencing their ethical decision-making. While values such as honesty and loyalty may be universally recognized, their relative importance and application may differ dramatically from culture to culture, leading to potential misunderstandings and ethical conflicts in intercultural contexts.

Also, the dynamic nature of values is influenced significantly by cultural context. In individualistic cultures, such as many Western societies, values often emphasize personal achievement, autonomy, and individual freedom. In contrast, collectivist cultures, prevalent in many parts of Asia and Africa, may prioritize values such as harmony, group belonging, and respect for elders. These cultural differences impact individual value hierarchies, influencing decision-making, interpersonal relationships, and overall life goals.

When different cultures prioritize values differently, ethical misunderstandings may occur. Traditionally, Korean society has emphasized loyalty and respect for authority above honesty, as demonstrated by an American professor who formerly taught at the South Korean Yonsei University:

> *In Korea as in the West, honesty and loyalty are both virtues. In the West, in general, honesty is the higher virtue. In a Confucian society like Korea, loyalty is the higher virtue . . . I had a terrible time in my classes when I was teaching at Yonsei because my students kept cheating on tests and plagiarizing homework . . . When I caught them, they were embarrassed, yes, and they knew they had done wrong, yes, but they said, "My friend asked me," as if that were a complete explanation . . .*
>
> *It is not the case that Koreans are dishonest. It is not the case that honesty is not a value in Korea. Korean culture has a strong sense of honesty. The problem is the hierarchy of values. Honesty is a value, but there is a higher value, and it is loyalty.*

We all make decisions each day, and we often prioritize one value over another without even realizing it. It's important to take cultural differences into consideration to avoid unfairly judging the choices of others from different cultures.

Values are not static; they evolve and change over time as individuals gain new experiences, encounter new perspectives, and grow. This is true in South Korea—while loyalty remains an important value there, the balance of values has shifted so that now there is an increased emphasis on honesty and integrity.

South Korean companies have taken significant steps to promote honesty and integrity within their organizations. For instance, Samsung Electronics, Hyundai Motor Group, and LG Electronics have implemented robust ethics programs, including codes of conduct, reporting mechanisms, and fair-trade initiatives. These companies recognize the importance of ethical behavior in maintaining their reputations and ensuring long-term success.

This evolution is driven by globalization, democratization, and the increasing influence of social media. There is a greater emphasis on personal rights and accountability, which has led to increased scrutiny of corporate behavior and a demand for greater transparency and ethical conduct.

THE ROLE OF SMARTPHONES, SOCIAL MEDIA, AND OTHER TECHNOLOGIES

The extensive use of smartphones and social media has led to a greater awareness of ethical standards and expectations and has fundamentally altered the global ethical landscape. With the ability of ordinary citizens to capture video, photographs, and audio and disseminate information instantaneously through social media and by other means, individuals now possess unprecedented power to document and expose wrongdoing. This is particularly beneficial in places where local customs discourage speaking out against corruption and other forms of dishonesty.

Increased transparency has significantly impacted the behavior of individuals and organizations alike. When employees document and share evidence of unsafe working conditions, such as inadequate safety measures or exploitative labor practices, companies are pressured to address the issues. Viral social media posts exposing wrongdoing, in many instances, lead to positive change.

One specific example is when, in 2018, a group of South Korean employees used social media to expose a company that was forcing its employees to work overtime without pay. This exposure led to positive change for these employees.

In 2016, a group of Korean journalists used social media to expose a massive corruption scandal in relation to the unusual access that Choi Soon-sil, the daughter of shaman-esque cult leader Choi Tae-min, had to South Korean President Park Geun-hye. This scandal led to Park's impeachment and removal from office.

This transformative power of citizen journalism, amplified by the reach of social media, was tragically exemplified in the Rana Plaza factory collapse.

CASE STUDY: THE RANA PLAZA TRAGEDY

In 2013, the Rana Plaza garment factory in Bangladesh collapsed, resulting in the deaths of more than 1,100 workers. This tragedy served as a stark reminder of the ethical complexities within global supply chains. While the tragedy highlighted the devastating consequences of prioritizing profit over worker safety, it also demonstrated the power of social media in exposing corporate wrongdoing and driving global change.

Social media platforms like Facebook and the platform formerly known as Twitter played a crucial role in disseminating information about the disaster to a global audience. Images and videos of the collapsed building and the plight of the affected workers quickly spread, sparking outrage and public outcry. Activists and concerned citizens used these platforms to organize campaigns, raise awareness, and demand accountability from brands who sourced garments from the factory. The Rana Plaza tragedy led to increased pressure on international brands to improve safety standards in their supply chains.

In addition, consumers, empowered by social media, began to boycott brands associated with the factory collapse, demanding greater transparency and ethical sourcing practices. This public pressure compelled many brands to sign the Accord on Fire and Building Safety in Bangladesh, a legally binding agreement that aims to improve safety conditions in garment factories.

KEY TAKEAWAYS

By embracing ethical principles and fostering a culture of integrity, businesses and individuals build trust, minimize risks, enhance their reputation, avoid impediments, and contribute to a more just and sustainable future.

Reflect on your organization's ethics practices. What are your strengths and weaknesses? How can you improve your organization's ethical practices and promote an ethical culture?

Chapter 9

GLOBAL SUPPLY CHAIN MANAGEMENT

In today's interconnected world, businesses rely on complex global supply chains to source materials, manufacture products, and distribute goods to customers. Effective global supply chain management is essential for ensuring business continuity, minimizing costs, and meeting customer expectations. This chapter explores the challenges and opportunities of managing global supply chains, along with strategies for doing so successfully.

GLOBAL SUPPLY CHAIN MANAGEMENT: CHALLENGES, OPPORTUNITIES, AND STRATEGIES

Global supply chains can be complex, involving multiple suppliers, manufacturers, and logistics providers located in different countries. For example, a company that manufactures electronics may have suppliers in Asia, Europe, and the Americas. This complexity may make it difficult to track products, identify and manage risks, and ensure that products are delivered on time and to the desired quality standards.

But global supply chains offer a wealth of opportunities for businesses to gain a competitive advantage. By strategically managing these complex networks, companies unlock significant value, enhance their resilience, and drive sustainable growth.

Risk Management

Global supply chains are exposed to various risks, including natural disasters, political instability, economic fluctuations, and transportation disruptions.

Businesses can reduce their exposure to risk by diversifying their supply chains. A company that relies on a single supplier is vulnerable to disruptions if that supplier experiences problems—diversifying your supply chain will reduce risk and ensure ongoing access to necessary materials and components. Creating and implementing contingency plans and purchasing insurance will also reduce risk.

Sustainability and Ethical Sourcing

Global supply chains significantly impact the environment and society. Businesses must ensure their suppliers comply with international standards and that their supply chains are sustainable and ethical. This includes addressing labor rights, including avoiding forced labor and child labor, and addressing climate change and other environmental concerns. For example, a company that uses palm oil in its products must ensure that it is sourced from sustainable plantations that do not contribute to deforestation.

Businesses can work with suppliers to help them implement sustainable practices and reduce their environmental impact and use third-party auditors to verify that their suppliers meet high ethical standards.

Cost Optimization

Leveraging global sourcing networks and sourcing from low-cost regions significantly reduces production costs by allowing businesses to access raw materials, components, and labor at competitive prices. Businesses can also reduce supply chain expenses by optimizing logistics, minimizing transportation costs, and streamlining inventory management.

In addition, building strong relationships with suppliers and leveraging their collective bargaining power to negotiate can lead to significant cost savings through favorable pricing agreements and improved contract terms.

Enhanced Customer Service

Globalized supply chains enable faster delivery times, meeting the increasing demands by today's consumers for rapid fulfillment and on-demand services.

By diversifying sourcing and leveraging global networks, businesses can ensure a consistent supply of products and minimize the risk of stockouts, enhancing customer satisfaction.

In addition, global supply chains provide access to new markets and customer segments, enabling businesses to expand their reach and increase their market share.

Innovation

Global supply chains serve as powerful incubators for innovation. By connecting businesses with suppliers and partners across diverse geographic and cultural landscapes, they facilitate the cross-pollination of ideas and best practices. For example, a company that sources materials from a supplier in a developing country may encounter novel production methods, innovative technologies, or unique approaches to problem-solving that can be adapted and applied to its own operations.

Furthermore, interacting with suppliers and partners from different cultural backgrounds can challenge existing assumptions and encourage creative thinking. Exposure to diverse perspectives and approaches can inspire new product designs, improve operational efficiency, and drive continuous innovation throughout the entire supply chain.

By leveraging the diverse knowledge and expertise within their global supply chains, businesses can gain a competitive edge, develop more sustainable and innovative solutions, and contribute to a more dynamic and interconnected global economy.

Technological Advancements

Rapid technological advancements are changing the global supply chain management landscape. Businesses must stay up to date on the latest technologies and trends to remain competitive and should leverage technology to improve their supply chain management. For example, blockchain technology can help companies track products throughout their supply chain and ensure they are not counterfeit.

Businesses may also use AI to optimize inventory levels and the Internet of Things (IoT) to monitor supply chain operations.

Maintaining Visibility

Maintaining visibility across the entire supply chain is paramount. Real-time data and insights are crucial for identifying potential risks, mitigating disruptions, and optimizing operations.

Leveraging advanced technologies such as IoT sensors, blockchain, and AI enables businesses to gain unprecedented visibility into their supply chains. This includes real-time tracking of shipments, monitoring of inventory levels, and proactive identification of potential disruptions such as natural disasters, political instability, or unforeseen demand fluctuations.

By harnessing the power of data analytics and predictive modeling, businesses can anticipate and proactively address potential challenges, minimize disruptions, and ensure the smooth and efficient flow of goods and services. This enhanced visibility not only improves operational efficiency but also strengthens relationships with suppliers and customers, builds trust, and ultimately enhances the overall resilience of the supply chain.

The following case study illustrates how Apple successfully applies these strategies to achieve great success. (See chapter 12 for a detailed discussion of technological advancements in global business.)

CASE STUDY: APPLE'S SUPPLY CHAIN STRATEGY

Apple, a global technology giant, maintains a complex and intricate supply chain that spans multiple continents. The company's success is underpinned by its ability to effectively manage this supply chain, ensuring the timely delivery of high-quality products to customers worldwide.

Given the global nature of its operations, Apple faces a range of potential risks, including natural disasters and geopolitical events, which may disrupt the supply chain. To mitigate these risks, Apple employs a dedicated team of experts who monitor global events and identify potential threats to its supply chain. By proactively seeking to anticipate these risks, Apple minimizes disruptions and ensures a continuous flow of products to its customers.

Another key strategy Apple implements is ensuring visibility and transparency throughout the supply chain. Using technologies such as radio frequency identification (RFID) tags, Apple tracks its products from manufacturing facility to retail store. This real-time visibility allows the company to monitor inventory levels, identify potential bottlenecks, and make data-driven decisions to optimize its supply chain.

In addition, Apple is committed to sustainability and corporate responsibility. The company has implemented various initiatives, such as using renewable energy, reducing waste, and promoting fair labor practices throughout its supply chain, to reduce its environmental impact. By focusing on sustainability, Apple is contributing to a healthier planet and building a positive reputation with consumers and stakeholders.

Finally, Apple recognizes the importance of collaboration and partnerships in managing its complex supply chain. The company works closely with its suppliers to improve efficiency, reduce costs, and ensure that products meet Apple's high standards for quality and sustainability. Apple has developed the "Supplier Code of Conduct," which outlines the expectations and standards that its suppliers must adhere to, promoting ethical and responsible business practices.

Apple's resilient and efficient supply chain strategy is a model for other global companies.

KEY TAKEAWAYS

Effective global supply chain management is essential for businesses today. By addressing challenges, seizing opportunities, and implementing effective strategies, companies will improve their efficiency and competitiveness, reduce costs, and enhance their sustainability.

Reflect on your organization's global supply chain management practices. What are your strengths and weaknesses? How can you improve your organization's supply chain management?

Chapter 10

GLOBAL MARKETING AND BRANDING

As a business expands operations into global markets, their marketing strategies will need to be adjusted. Effective international marketing requires a deep understanding of cultural differences, consumer preferences, and market dynamics.

This chapter explores the challenges and opportunities of marketing products and services in diverse global markets and discusses important considerations when it comes to brand localization and cultural adaptation.

GLOBAL STANDARDIZATION AND GLOCALIZATION

Adopting a standardized global brand identity, emphasizing consistency and uniformity across all markets, can be effective for brands with strong worldwide recognition and a consistent product offering. But adapting your brand and messaging may also be necessary—effective global branding requires balancing consistency and adaptation.

As your company enters new markets, in addition to considering the different regulations and standards in each country, you'll want to conduct thorough market research to understand the unique needs and preferences of consumers. Then you'll be able to tailor brand messaging and positioning to resonate with the specific values, aspirations, and lifestyles of target audiences in each market. In addition, partnering with local agencies and cultural experts will help to ensure that your marketing campaigns are culturally sensitive and effective.

Glocalization is combining global standardization with local adaptation to create a globally recognizable and locally relevant brand. Glocalization allows brands to maintain a consistent brand identity while adapting to different markets' unique needs and preferences. This may involve changing product features, packaging, or flavors. For example, food companies often adapt their products' flavors to suit the tastes of different cultures. And car manufacturers often adapt their vehicles to suit different markets' specific needs and preferences, such as offering vehicles with stronger air conditioning systems and different engine cooling systems in countries with hot climates, and vehicles with more powerful engines and improved traction control in countries with mountainous terrain.

As you consider your global marketing strategies, here are some other market considerations.

Language

Be mindful of different language and cultural nuances when producing marketing messages and materials and ensure accurate and culturally appropriate translation. Utilize local colloquialisms and cultural references so that marketing messages resonate with target audiences.

For example, a global brand might adapt their company name or use different taglines in different markets to appeal to local preferences.

Values, Beliefs, Symbols, and Imagery

Respect and understand the values and beliefs of target audiences in each market. Use symbols and imagery that are culturally appropriate and resonate with target audiences. Avoid using symbols or imagery that have negative connotations or could be considered offensive or disrespectful.

For example, in some East Asian cultures, the number *four* is considered unlucky as it sounds the same or similar to the word for "death." Therefore, brands should avoid using the number four prominently in marketing materials intended for these markets. Some elevator companies substitute the number four with the letter *F* or completely skip that number. And some high-rise buildings provide a garden or recreation space on the fourth floor so that no one has to live or work on that floor.

In Western cultures, red is often associated with passion, energy, and success. It's frequently used in marketing campaigns to convey excitement and urgency. In many Asian cultures, red is associated with good fortune and prosperity. Conversely, red can be associated with mourning or danger in some African cultures.

Local Representation

In advertising campaigns, it may be advantageous to utilize professional models and actors native to the target market, featuring individuals who represent the diversity of the target audience. Employing voice actors who are native speakers of the local language for audio content may also be prudent.

EPRG MODEL

As you make marketing decisions in different markets, it's helpful to consider the EPRG framework. This model outlines four primary orientations that guide international marketing strategies: ethnocentric, polycentric, regiocentric, and geocentric. Each approach represents a different balance between global standardization and local adaptation, directly impacting how brands interact with diverse markets.

While a geocentric approach is preferred, other approaches may be suitable for less-established organizations. Understanding these orientations will provide a clearer lens through which to analyze potential global marketing strategies.

Ethnocentric Approach

An ethnocentric approach to marketing is when home country practices, values, and strategies dominate. The business sees its domestic way as the "right" way.

Scalability:

- centralized decision-making
- products and marketing often replicated with minimal local adaptation
- often used in early stages of expansion or by companies with limited international experience

Pros:

- consistency in brand and operations
- cost-effective due to economies of scale

Cons:

- can lead to cultural insensitivity
- often ineffective in diverse or complex markets

Polycentric Approach

A polycentric approach to marketing is when each host country is treated as unique and local subsidiaries have autonomy.

Scalability:

- decentralized structure
- strategies, products, and marketing tailored for local markets

Pros:

- high local relevance
- strong local relationships and responsiveness

Cons:

- expensive to scale
- risk of brand inconsistency
- less control and coordination

Regiocentric Approach

With a regiocentric approach, strategies are regionally focused, grouping countries with similar characteristics.

Scalability:

- semi-centralized
- services and resources shared at the regional level

Pros:

- balances efficiency and customization
- easier regional coordination

Cons:

- regional differences may still be vast
- may overlook global standardization opportunities

Geocentric (Global) Approach

A geocentric approach, when feasible, is the ideal approach to global marketing. With this approach, organizations think globally and act locally. Decisions and strategies are integrated across the business, regardless of which country you're doing business in.

Scalability:

- centralized core with localized execution
- knowledge and talent flow in all directions

Pros:

- efficient use of global resources
- strong brand consistency with local relevance

Cons:

- complex to manage
- high cost of coordination and integration

By strategically applying the EPRG framework, businesses can navigate the complexities of global marketing, ensuring their brands resonate with diverse audiences while maintaining a cohesive global identity.

As the following case studies about Coca-Cola, IKEA, and

McDonald's illustrate, successful global brands often adopt a geocentric approach, balancing global brand consistency with necessary local adaptations. Their strategies demonstrate a keen understanding of cultural nuances and consumer preferences, reflecting the "think globally, act locally" mantra.

Conversely, the Dolce & Gabbana example serves as a cautionary tale of the risks associated with an ethnocentric or poorly executed polycentric approach, where cultural insensitivity can lead to significant repercussions.

CASE STUDY: COCA-COLA—A TIMELESS BRAND, EVOLVING GLOBALLY

Coca-Cola, one of the world's most recognizable brands, has been successfully navigating diverse cultural contexts for more than a century. The company's iconic red can and the familiar Coca-Cola logo have become global symbols of refreshment and happiness. While maintaining its brand identity, Coca-Cola has tailored its marketing campaigns, product offerings, and packaging to appeal to different audiences. For example, Coca-Cola often utilizes local celebrities in their advertising to have greater appeal in specific markets. In India, they partnered with local NGOs to promote women's empowerment and community development, aligning with the country's cultural values.

In some markets, Coca-Cola has introduced unique flavors (such as Vanilla Coke, Coke Lime, Coca-Cola Raspberry, and Coca-Cola Zero Sugar) and limited-edition products (such as Coca-Cola Oreo Zero Sugar, Coca-Cola Y3000, Coca-Cola Dreamworld, and Coca-Cola

Move) to cater to specific preferences. Coca-Cola's culturally sensitive strategy has helped them remain relevant and appealing to consumers in diverse markets.

CASE STUDY: IKEA'S CULTURAL ADAPTATION

IKEA, the Swedish furniture giant, exemplifies successful global expansion through careful cultural adaptation. While maintaining its core brand identity of minimalist design and affordability, IKEA strategically adjusts its product offerings and marketing strategies to resonate with local preferences and cultural nuances.

For example, in China, IKEA uses the company name *Yijia Jiaju* instead of a name that sounds more like *Ikea. Yijia Jiaju* roughly means "affordable home furnishings." The name is frequently shortened to just the first word, *Yijia*, which has cultural significance because it comes from an ancient Chinese poem that celebrates happy marriage and home life. The company has maintained the core essence of its message while adapting the company name to better connect with the local culture.

In Japan, where living spaces are typically small, IKEA offers compact furniture and home furnishings designed to maximize space utilization. In India, IKEA appeals to local aesthetics by incorporating traditional Indian motifs and colors into some of its product lines.

In the Middle East, IKEA adapts its advertising campaigns to align with local cultural norms and values. Recognizing the importance of family and community in these cultures, IKEA shifted its focus from individualistic themes of self-expression to emphasizing the role of home as a gathering place for family and friends. For example, instead of solely focusing on sleek, minimalist aesthetics, IKEA's marketing campaigns in the Middle East emphasize the creation of warm and inviting home environments where families come together to relax, entertain, and celebrate. Advertisements feature images of families enjoying meals together around dining tables, children playing in cozy living rooms, and extended families gathering for festive occasions.

By carefully considering the unique needs and preferences of consumers in each market, IKEA has successfully established a strong global presence while maintaining its core brand identity.

CASE STUDY: MCDONALD'S—A GLOBAL ICON, TAILORED LOCALLY

McDonald's, another global branding success story, has demonstrated a remarkable ability to adapt to different cultural contexts. While maintaining its core brand identity, McDonald's customizes its menus and marketing campaigns to cater to local tastes and preferences.

For example, in Japan, McDonald's offers a variety of teriyaki burgers and other Japanese-inspired dishes. In India, where a large percentage of the population does not eat beef and many people are vegetarian, they don't serve any beef and they offer a variety of vegetarian options. In countries in the Middle East where the majority of the population is Muslim, McDonald's food is 100 percent halal. In China, McDonald's has altered their global tagline, "I'm Lovin' It," to "Delicious!" which better resonates with Chinese cultural preferences for concise and direct communication.

McDonald's has also successfully built strong relationships with local communities and suppliers. The company partners with local farmers and businesses to support the economy. This approach has helped McDonald's to be seen as a responsible corporate citizen in many countries.

McDonald's global marketing campaigns aren't always successful. For instance, on one occasion when McDonald's commented on the platform formerly known as Twitter that in India, a country where about 80 percent of the population is Hindu (not Muslim), their food is halal certified, there was a strong public sentiment that McDonald's had been culturally insensitive. As a result, many people boycotted the fast food chain.

Dolce & Gabbana had a similar blunder, as described in the following case study.

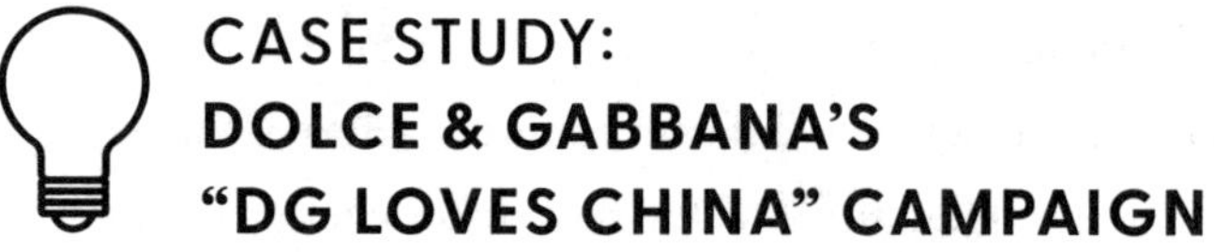

CASE STUDY: DOLCE & GABBANA'S "DG LOVES CHINA" CAMPAIGN

In 2018, Italian luxury fashion house Dolce & Gabbana launched a highly controversial advertising campaign in China. The campaign featured a Chinese model struggling to eat Italian food with chopsticks, accompanied by the hashtag #DGLovesChina. This perceived stereotyping and cultural insensitivity sparked outrage among Chinese consumers and social media users.

The campaign quickly went viral on Chinese social media platforms, with many users accusing the brand of racism and cultural appropriation. Chinese celebrities and influencers publicly denounced the campaign, and online retailers pulled Dolce & Gabbana products from their platforms. The backlash led to the cancellation of a highly anticipated fashion show in Shanghai, resulting in significant financial losses for the brand.

This example serves as a stark reminder of the importance of conducting thorough market research, consulting with cultural experts, and ensuring that marketing is sensitive to the local culture. Failing to understand and appreciate the nuances of a particular culture can have severe consequences, including reputational damage, financial loss, and boycotts.

KEY TAKEAWAYS

Global marketing requires a deep understanding of cultural nuances and a willingness to adapt to market dynamics. By developing a solid brand identity; customizing products, services, and messaging; and building relationships with local partners, businesses can successfully navigate global markets and achieve long-term success. The EPRG framework offers a strategic lens to analyze and implement global marketing strategies, highlighting the importance of balancing global standardization with local adaptation.

Reflect on your organization's global marketing strategy. How effectively is your brand positioned in different markets? Which EPRG orientation best aligns with your current and future goals? What are the key challenges you face in your international marketing efforts? What changes to your global marketing strategy would benefit your organization?

Chapter 11

EMERGING MARKETS

As enterprises expand their global reach, expanding into emerging markets is a great opportunity for many. This chapter explores the unique characteristics of emerging markets, the opportunities and challenges they present, and strategies for successful business operations in these regions.

CHARACTERISTICS OF EMERGING MARKETS

What is an emerging market? Here are some common characteristics:

- **Rapid economic growth:** Emerging markets are typically characterized by rapid economic expansion driven by factors such as industrialization, technological advancements, and increasing urbanization. These economies often transition from primarily agricultural or resource-based economies toward economies with more diversified and industrialized structures, leading to significant economic and social transformation.

- **A large and growing consumer base:** The rapid economic growth of emerging markets creates a large and growing consumer base with increasing purchasing power.
- **Increasing globalization and diverse cultural and social landscapes:** Fueled by technological advancements and increased global interconnectedness, emerging markets are characterized by diverse cultural and social landscapes. These markets often exhibit a rich tapestry of cultures, languages, religions, and social norms, creating a complex and dynamic business environment.
- **Infrastructure development:** Many emerging markets are experiencing rapid infrastructure development, including improvements in transportation, telecommunications, and energy.
- **Innovation and entrepreneurship:** Emerging markets are often characterized by a vibrant entrepreneurial culture and a focus on innovation.
- **Political and economic instability:** Emerging markets are often subject to political and economic instability.

The following countries are often considered emerging markets:

- **Africa:** the Democratic Republic of the Congo, Nigeria, and South Africa
- **Asia:** China, Hong Kong, India, Indonesia, Malaysia, the Philippines, Singapore, South Korea, Taiwan, Thailand, and Vietnam
- **Eastern Europe:** the Czech Republic, Hungary, Poland, Romania, and Russia
- **Latin America:** Argentina, Brazil, Chile, Colombia, Mexico, and Peru

- **Middle East:** Egypt, Saudi Arabia, Turkey, and the UAE

Note: This list is not exhaustive and there is no single, universally accepted definition of an "emerging market." Also, some of these countries are considered "frontier markets," which are considered to be riskier than emerging markets.

The classification of countries as emerging markets changes over time based on economic growth, political stability, and other factors.

OPPORTUNITIES IN EMERGING MARKETS

Emerging markets present many opportunities for global mindset leadership, including some of the following.

Market Growth

As emerging markets develop, a growing middle class emerges, characterized by increasing disposable income and a demand for consumer goods and services. This expanding consumer base presents significant opportunities for businesses to capture market share and achieve rapid growth.

Lower Labor Costs

Emerging markets often have lower labor costs than developed economies, making them attractive locations for manufacturing and outsourcing facilities. The low labor costs help businesses reduce costs and improve their competitiveness.

Innovation and Entrepreneurship

The entrepreneurial culture often present in emerging markets creates opportunities for businesses to develop new products and services and capture market share.

Resource Abundance

Many emerging markets are rich in natural resources, creating opportunities for businesses in the extractive industries. However, ensuring these resources are extracted sustainably and responsibly rather than exploited is essential.

Infrastructure Development

Improvements in transportation, telecommunications, and energy create new business opportunities and improve the overall business environment. For example, expanding transportation networks, such as roads, railways, and airports, facilitate the movement of goods and people, while advancements in telecommunications infrastructure, such as increased internet penetration and mobile connectivity, enhance business operations and facilitate e-commerce. These infrastructure improvements support economic growth and improve citizens' quality of life in emerging markets.

CHALLENGES OF OPERATING IN EMERGING MARKETS

Emerging markets, while offering significant growth opportunities, also present unique challenges. Here are a few.

Political Instability

The political instability common in emerging markets may manifest in various forms, including political upheaval, changes in government policies, and geopolitical tensions. These factors may create uncertainty for businesses, leading to disruptions in operations, difficulties in enforcing contracts, and increased risks for investors. For example, sudden policy changes, such as changes in trade regulations or tax laws, may significantly impact business operations.

Many African countries, such as the Democratic Republic of the Congo, are currently politically unstable, and many countries in Latin America are experiencing ongoing political challenges.

Economic Instability

Economic instability may also pose significant challenges for businesses operating in emerging markets. Rapid economic growth in emerging markets is sometimes accompanied by high inflation, currency fluctuations, increased volatility in financial markets, and unpredictable consumer spending. These factors create uncertainty for businesses and may impact their profitability and long-term sustainability.

Examples include the devastating economic crises experienced in some emerging European economies during the 2008 financial crisis and the prolonged economic stagnation that has hampered growth in many Latin American countries.

Regulatory Challenges

Businesses must be aware of and comply with local laws and regulations, which vary significantly from country to country. Navigating the complex regulatory environments in emerging markets can be challenging.

Infrastructure Limitations

Inadequate infrastructure may hinder business operations and increase costs. This may include challenges with transportation, energy, and telecommunications.

Corruption and Bribery

Corruption and bribery are a significant challenge in some emerging markets. Businesses need to be aware of the risks of corruption and take steps to prevent it.

Social and Environmental Risks

Emerging markets may face challenges related to social unrest, environmental issues (such as air pollution, depleted water and soil, destruction of ecosystems, and extinction of wildlife), and health concerns. These factors may impact business operations and create reputational risks.

Cultural Differences

Diverse cultural and social landscapes with varying values, beliefs, and behaviors often characterize emerging markets, making business decisions more complex for business owners.

Undereducated or Inexperienced Workforce

The workforce in an emerging market may lack the necessary skills and experience to meet the demands of modern businesses, requiring significant investments in training and development.

Health and Safety Risks

Employees operating in emerging markets may face increased risks of infectious diseases, natural disasters, and other health and safety hazards.

By carefully assessing and mitigating these challenges, businesses increase their chances of success in these dynamic and rapidly evolving markets.

STRATEGIES FOR SUCCESS IN EMERGING MARKETS

When considering entering an emerging market, it is essential to conduct thorough market research to understand the risks and opportunities as well as consumers' needs and preferences. Your market research will help you proactively mitigate risks, tailor your products and services to meet local demand, and capitalize on growth potential while navigating the inherent challenges.

The following strategies are helpful to employ when entering an emerging market.

Form Local Partnerships and Engage with the Local Community

Partner with local businesses and organizations to gain insights into the local market and build relationships with key stakeholders. Build strong relationships in local communities and address their concerns. This can help you navigate the complexities of the local business environment and avoid common pitfalls.

Be Culturally Sensitive

Understanding and adapting to diverse cultural and social contexts is essential for success in emerging markets. In order to build trust with local partners and consumers, it's important to demonstrate cultural sensitivity and respect for local values, customs, and traditions and adapt marketing and communication strategies to resonate with local audiences.

Manage Risks

Companies should conduct thorough risk assessments in emerging markets they plan to enter, then develop robust risk management strategies, such as the following, to mitigate the risks.

Purchase Political Risk Insurance

In politically unstable markets, strategically acquiring political risk insurance is not merely a precautionary measure but a critical component of safeguarding long-term investments and operational continuity. This insurance acts as a vital shield against potential catastrophic losses stemming from political instability, including expropriation, political violence, and currency devaluation.

By proactively mitigating these risks, businesses can maintain investor confidence, protect valuable assets, and ensure the resilience of their global operations in volatile environments.

Currency Hedging

In emerging markets, currency fluctuations are a constant challenge for businesses. Strategic currency hedging is crucial for protecting profit margins, ensuring financial stability, and maintaining competitive pricing.

By proactively managing currency risk through tools like forward contracts, options, or swaps, companies can minimize the adverse effects of volatile exchange rates and enhance their long-term financial planning.

Develop Robust Contingency Plans

Strategically constructing robust contingency plans helps ensure organizational resilience and will help you maintain a competitive edge in an unpredictable global landscape. These plans serve as a critical strategic framework, enabling businesses to swiftly adapt and minimize disruptions caused by unforeseen events such as natural disasters, political unrest, or complex supply chain breakdowns.

By anticipating potential vulnerabilities and outlining clear, actionable responses, organizations can safeguard their operational continuity, protect stakeholder value, and navigate turbulent environments with confidence.

Prioritize Employee Safety and Well-Being

Strategically prioritizing employee safety and well-being in emerging markets is, of course, a matter of ethical responsibility but also a fundamental pillar for sustainable global operations and long-term success. Implementing robust health and safety protocols is a critical strategic investment that safeguards human capital, enhances employee morale, and mitigates potential operational disruptions.

By fostering a culture of care and demonstrating a genuine commitment to employee well-being, organizations build trust, attract top talent, and cultivate a resilient workforce capable of navigating the unique challenges of emerging market environments.

Security Measures

Strategically implementing comprehensive security measures is not merely a defensive tactic but a proactive investment in safeguarding critical assets and ensuring long-term organizational stability. Robust security protocols, designed to protect employees, physical assets, and intellectual property, are essential for mitigating risks, maintaining operational continuity, and preserving competitive advantage in an increasingly volatile global landscape.

To achieve this, organizations can implement a range of security measures, including the following, as appropriate for your organization.

Physical Security

- Install advanced surveillance systems such as CCTV cameras with real-time monitoring and recording capabilities.
- Implement access control systems, including biometric scanners, keycard entry, and security checkpoints, to deter intrusions and restrict unauthorized access to sensitive areas.
- Deploy alarm systems and motion sensors to detect and deter intrusions.
- Hire and train a professional security team, including on-site guards and security personnel, to patrol premises and respond to security incidents.

Cybersecurity

- Implement robust firewalls, intrusion detection systems, and antivirus software to protect against cyber threats.
- Conduct regular security audits and vulnerability assessments to identify and address potential weaknesses in IT infrastructure.
- Encrypt data and utilize secure data storage solutions to protect sensitive information.
- Train employees on cybersecurity best practices, including phishing awareness and password management.

Intellectual Property Protection

- Implement strict confidentiality agreements and nondisclosure agreements with employees and partners.
- Secure document management systems and access controls to protect sensitive research and development data.
- Regularly monitor and enforce intellectual property rights, including patents, trademarks, and copyrights.
- Implement security measures to protect trade secrets.

By prioritizing security as a strategic imperative and implementing these types of comprehensive measures, organizations build trust with stakeholders, protect their reputations, and foster a secure environment conducive to innovation and sustainable growth.

Operate Sustainably

Consider the sustainability implications of your business operations in emerging markets. By operating sustainably, you can build a positive reputation and enhance your long-term competitiveness, create a positive and lasting impact on the long-term development of the communities in which you operate, and attract and retain top talent. Key sustainability considerations include the following:

- **Environmental Impact:** Minimize your ecological footprint by reducing waste, conserving energy, and promoting sustainable sourcing practices. Also, look for opportunities to support local environmental initiatives.
- **Social Impact:** Support local communities through job creation, skills development programs, and community investment.
- **Ethical Sourcing:** Ensure that your supply chains are free from exploitation and that all workers are treated fairly and ethically.

CASE STUDY: TATA CONSULTANCY SERVICES (TCS) EXPANDING GLOBALLY

India is one of the world's largest and fastest-growing economies, offering significant business opportunities. The country's large and diverse population, growing middle class, and favorable government policies have made it an attractive destination for foreign investment. However, infrastructure limitations, corruption, and regulatory complexities may make it difficult for businesses to operate there.

A leading multinational company based in India, Tata Consultancy Services (TCS) exemplifies the successful navigation of the Indian market and demonstrates how a global mindset drives success in emerging economies.

TCS is a services-based IT corporation with many clients across several industries, including government, BFSI (Banking, Financial Services, and Insurance), manufacturing, retail, and telecom. Some of TCS's prominent clients include General Electric, Morgan Stanley, SBI (State Bank of India), UBC (University of British Columbia), Jaguar Land Rover, Fidelity, and Vodafone India.

TCS deeply understands the Indian market and has built its foundation within the country. This deep understanding and market research allows them to anticipate market trends, identify emerging opportunities, and tailor their services to meet the specific needs of Indian businesses and consumers.

Also, TCS has cultivated strong relationships and partnerships with local businesses, government agencies, and academic institutions. These partnerships provide valuable insights into the local market, facilitate access to resources, and enhance their ability to navigate the complexities of the Indian business environment.

In addition, TCS recognizes the importance of cultural sensitivity in the Indian market. The company has successfully integrated Indian cultural values and traditions into its business practices, fostering strong relationships with clients and employees.

TCS has proactively addressed the challenges of operating in the Indian market, including navigating political and regulatory complexities. The company has mitigated risk by investing heavily in building a robust and resilient infrastructure, ensuring business continuity despite challenges that may arise in the future.

TCS is committed to sustainability, integrating environmental and social responsibility into its business operations. The company has implemented initiatives to reduce its carbon footprint, promote employee well-being, and support local communities through various social impact programs.

Building upon its success in the Indian market, TCS has expanded globally. The Tata Group is India's largest business conglomerate, with operations in more than 100 countries. By leveraging its deep understanding of the Indian market and applying this knowledge to other emerging markets, TCS has become a global leader in the IT services industry. TCS's success demonstrates how a global mindset, characterized by cultural sensitivity, adaptability, and commitment to sustainability, is crucial for success in today's interconnected world.

KEY TAKEAWAYS

Emerging markets present businesses with both opportunities and challenges. Companies can successfully navigate emerging markets and capitalize on their growth potential by understanding their unique characteristics, conducting thorough market research, and developing effective strategies.

Reflect on your organization's experience operating in emerging markets. What challenges have you faced? What strategies have you found to be effective? How can your organization improve its operations in emerging markets?

Or, if your organization has not yet expanded into an emerging market, consider the pros and cons, challenges and opportunities, of doing so. Which emerging market would provide the greatest opportunity or be the best fit for your organization? What is the next step to analyze the viability of expanding into that region? What strategies should you implement to maximize your potential to be successful?

SECTION 3

INNOVATION

Chapter 12

THE DIGITAL TRANSFORMATION OF GLOBAL BUSINESS

Digital technologies have revolutionized businesses' operations, transforming industries, creating new opportunities, and reshaping the global business landscape. Leaders must be agile and adaptable, equipped with the latest technology tools to succeed in a globalized world.

This chapter discusses the profound impact of the digital transformation on international business, examining key trends, challenges, and strategies for success.

CASE STUDY: AMAZON—A DIGITAL TRANSFORMATION SUCCESS STORY

Once a small online bookstore, Amazon has transformed into a global e-commerce giant, leveraging digital technologies to revolutionize the retail industry. Its success story serves as a testament to the power of digital transformation.

Amazon's early focus on e-commerce laid the foundation for its success. By establishing a user-friendly online platform, offering a vast selection of products, and providing competitive prices, Amazon quickly captured the attention of online shoppers globally. The company's innovative features, such as one-click ordering and customer reviews, further enhance the shopping experience for customers worldwide.

Amazon's foray into cloud computing with Amazon Web Services (AWS) has also helped drive its growth. AWS provides scalable cloud computing infrastructure, allowing businesses of all sizes across the globe to access computing resources without substantial up-front investment. This has enabled Amazon to tap into a new revenue stream and position itself as a leader in the global cloud computing market.

Amazon has been at the forefront of adopting AI and machine learning technologies. These technologies enable Amazon to personalize product recommendations, optimize global supply chains, and improve customer service. For example, Amazon's recommendation engine uses AI to analyze customer purchase history and preferences to suggest relevant products.

Amazon's efficient supply chain management has also been a critical factor in its success. The company has invested heavily in logistics infrastructure, including warehouses, fulfillment centers, and transportation networks. By leveraging technology and data analytics, Amazon has optimized its global supply chain, reduced costs, and improved delivery times.

Amazon has always prioritized customer satisfaction. The company's focus on providing excellent customer service, including easy returns, fast shipping, and responsive customer support, has helped it build a loyal, worldwide customer base. Amazon's commitment to customer experience has been a critical differentiator in the competitive global e-commerce market.

Despite its success, Amazon faces challenges. Increasing competition from other e-commerce giants, regulatory scrutiny, and the ethical implications of AI are some of the critical challenges that Amazon must address. However, the company's strong foundation, innovative culture, and financial resources position it well to navigate these challenges and capitalize on future opportunities.

Amazon's journey from a small online bookstore to one of the largest retailers in the world, selling to customers in more than 100 countries, is a testament to the power of digital transformation. By leveraging e-commerce, cloud computing, and AI, Amazon has revolutionized the retail industry and created a new model for business success. As the digital landscape continues to evolve, Amazon's ability to adapt and innovate will be crucial for maintaining its leadership position.

DIGITAL TRENDS

Over the last few decades, since the 1990s when owning a computer became common and the internet became publicly available, and the 2010s when owning a smartphone became common, the global exchange of information, goods, and services has grown exponentially, revolutionizing the hyperconnected world. In addition, technology has become a powerful tool for overcoming challenges in global business. Various software programs and tools are available to assist with translation, video conferencing, and project management. By leveraging these technologies, individuals and organizations can enhance communication, collaboration, and efficiency in a globalized environment.

In the pages that follow, we discuss key digital trends important to global business.

E-commerce

As illustrated by the Amazon case study, e-commerce enables businesses to reach customers worldwide, creating new markets and opportunities for growth. Online marketplaces, social media platforms, and mobile commerce have become essential channels for businesses to connect with consumers.

Remote Work

The increasing adoption of remote work technologies has enabled businesses to operate more flexibly and efficiently. Remote work can reduce overhead costs, improve employee satisfaction, and attract top talent from a global pool of workers. Companies like Google and Microsoft have embraced remote work policies, allowing employees to work from anywhere worldwide.

Democratization of Content Creation

Consider YouTube, a platform that allows anyone with a smartphone and internet connection to create and share video content. YouTubers like Mr. Beast have leveraged this platform to build massive followings and generate significant revenue through advertising and sponsorships, even before starting their own product lines. This empowers individuals to become entrepreneurs and build global followings without the traditional barriers to entry.

Social Media

Social media platforms like LinkedIn have revolutionized professional networking, allowing individuals to connect with colleagues and potential employers worldwide. Platforms like TikTok significantly influence purchasing decisions globally. Trending content and product placements spark viral sensations and drive sales for savvy businesses.

Online Reviews

User-generated reviews on platforms like Google and Yelp empower consumers and can make or break a business or product's reputation. Businesses must prioritize customer satisfaction and actively manage their online presence to build trust and attract customers.

Global Call Centers

The rise of global call centers allows businesses to provide 24/7 customer support at a lower cost. This ensures customer inquiries are addressed promptly, regardless of location, enhancing customer satisfaction and brand loyalty.

Internet of Things (IoT)

The IoT connects physical devices, vehicles, and buildings to the internet, enabling the collection and exchange of data. For example, IoT sensors can monitor inventory levels, track assets, and optimize energy consumption. This technology improves efficiency, optimizes supply chains, and creates new business models.

Big Data

The exponential growth of data has created opportunities for businesses to gain valuable insights and make data-driven decisions. Big data analytics tools can analyze large datasets and identify trends, patterns, and opportunities. For example, retailers can use big data to analyze customer purchasing behavior in a particular country and personalize marketing campaigns in that market.

Blockchain

Blockchain technology has the transformative potential to effectively address real-world challenges and create a more equitable global economy.

In traditional supply chains, tracking the origin and journey of products may be complex and prone to fraud. This lack of transparency may inadvertently lead to serious ethical concerns, such as forced labor, environmental damage, and the proliferation of counterfeit goods. For example, ensuring the safety and ethical sourcing of ingredients can be a significant challenge in the food industry.

Blockchain technology offers a powerful solution to these challenges by providing an immutable and transparent product origin and movement record. By recording every supply chain step on a secure and decentralized blockchain network, companies enhance traceability, improve product safety, and address ethical concerns.

For example, Walmart has implemented a blockchain-based system to track the origin of leafy greens. This system allows consumers to easily trace the product to the farm where it was grown, providing valuable information about its origin and ensuring that it meets safety and quality standards.

Nestlé also leverages blockchain technology to enhance the traceability of its coffee beans. By tracking the beans from farm to cup, Nestlé ensures that farmers receive fair compensation and that the coffee is sourced sustainably and ethically.

Beyond food, blockchain technology can be applied to various industries, including pharmaceuticals, fashion, and electronics, to improve supply chain transparency, reduce fraud, and enhance consumer trust. By leveraging the power of blockchain, companies build more ethical and sustainable supply chains while improving their brand reputation and enhancing consumer confidence.

Decentralized Finance (DeFi)

Millions of people worldwide lack access to traditional financial services such as bank accounts, loans, and insurance. This "financial exclusion" limits economic opportunities, hinders development, and perpetuates poverty.

DeFi applications leverage blockchain technology to provide underserved populations with access to financial services such as loans, insurance, and remittances. Unlike traditional banking systems, which often require extensive documentation and credit history, DeFi platforms operate on a decentralized and permissionless basis.

Lending and Borrowing

Platforms like Aave and Compound allow users to lend and borrow cryptocurrencies without intermediaries such as banks. This provides access to credit for individuals and businesses in emerging markets who may not qualify for traditional loans or lack access to formal banking systems. For example, farmers in remote regions can access loans to invest in their crops, while small businesses can secure expansion funding without bank approval.

Microfinance and Remittances

DeFi platforms can facilitate microfinance loans, enabling individuals and small businesses in developing countries to access small loans for business ventures or personal needs. Furthermore, DeFi platforms streamline cross-border remittances, reducing transaction costs and enabling faster and more affordable transfers of funds to family and friends in other countries.

Decentralized Insurance

DeFi platforms are also exploring innovative insurance models, such as decentralized insurance protocols that pool risk and provide coverage for various events such as crop failures, natural disasters, and cyberattacks.

While still in its early stages, DeFi has the potential to revolutionize access to financial services, empowering individuals and communities worldwide. By removing intermediaries and leveraging the transparency and efficiency of blockchain technology, DeFi contributes to a more inclusive and equitable financial system. However, it's crucial to acknowledge the challenges and risks associated with DeFi, such as price volatility, security vulnerabilities, and the lack of regulatory oversight.

Artificial Intelligence (AI)

AI is another important digital trend. AI has rapidly evolved from a futuristic concept to a transformative force shaping the global landscape.

In the pages that follow, we discuss the implications of increased AI utilization for individuals and businesses and the ethical considerations surrounding its development and deployment.

Automation and Efficiency

AI-powered automation is streamlining operations across industries, leading to higher productivity, reduced labor costs, and improved product quality.

In manufacturing, AI-enabled robots perform tasks such as assembly, welding, and quality control with precision and speed, surpassing human capabilities in many areas. This increased efficiency leads to higher productivity, reduced labor costs, and improved product quality.

In customer service, AI-powered chatbots handle routine inquiries and provide 24/7 support, freeing human agents to focus on more complex issues. Chatbots can provide personal recommendations, resolve customer complaints, and process orders, improving customer satisfaction and reducing operational costs.

Fraud Detection

AI is revolutionizing fraud detection by analyzing vast amounts of data to identify patterns and anomalies indicative of fraudulent activity. Machine learning algorithms can analyze transaction histories, user behavior, and other relevant data points to detect suspicious activity in real time. For example, AI can identify unusual spending patterns, such as sudden increases in transaction volume or purchases made from unusual locations. It can also detect anomalies in user behavior, such as multiple login attempts from different locations or changes in device information.

By continuously learning and adapting to new fraud tactics, AI-powered systems can effectively prevent and mitigate fraud across various domains, including financial transactions, online security, and insurance claims.

Data-Driven Decision-Making

AI's ability to analyze vast amounts of data empowers businesses, giving them valuable insights for informed decision-making. Retailers leverage AI to analyze customer data and personalize marketing campaigns, tailoring recommendations to individual preferences and increasing conversion rates.

AI significantly benefits supply chain management. AI-powered systems can optimize demand forecasting, inventory management, and transportation logistics, reducing costs, improving customer satisfaction, and reducing environmental impact. For example, AI can predict demand fluctuations, optimize transportation routes, and identify opportunities for cost savings.

Product Development

AI accelerates product development by automating design, testing, and prototyping tasks. AI-powered design tools are able to generate innovative designs based on customer preferences and market trends, reducing time-to-market. Additionally, AI can simulate product performance under various conditions, identifying potential flaws before production, thus improving product quality and reducing costs.

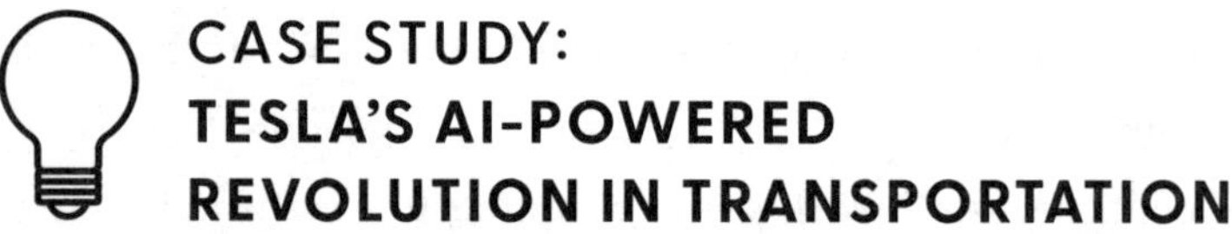

CASE STUDY: TESLA'S AI-POWERED REVOLUTION IN TRANSPORTATION

Tesla, the electric vehicle pioneer, has been at the forefront of using AI to transform the transportation industry. One of Tesla's most ambitious projects is the development of fully autonomous vehicles designed to navigate roads, detect obstacles, and make driving decisions without human intervention.

Tesla's AI systems rely on a vast network of sensors and cameras to gather data about the surrounding environment. This data is then processed by powerful AI algorithms that identify objects, interpret traffic signs, and predict the behavior of other vehicles. By analyzing this data in real time, Tesla's AI systems make decisions about steering, acceleration, braking, and driving maneuvers.

The potential benefits of Tesla's AI-powered self-driving technology are significant. Fully autonomous vehicles could dramatically improve road safety by reducing the number of accidents caused by human error. They could also help to alleviate traffic congestion by optimizing traffic flow and reducing the need for personal car ownership. Additionally, self-driving cars provide greater mobility for individuals who are unable to drive themselves, such as the elderly or people who are disabled.

While Tesla has made significant progress in developing self-driving technology, there are still significant challenges to overcome. Ensuring the safety and reliability of autonomous vehicles requires extensive testing and validation. Additionally, regulatory hurdles and public acceptance must be addressed before self-driving cars can become widely adopted.

Despite these challenges, Tesla's AI-powered self-driving technology has the potential to revolutionize transportation. By pushing the boundaries of innovation, Tesla is paving the way for a future where cars are not just vehicles but intelligent agents that help us navigate the world safely and efficiently.

AI and Global Markets

Market Expansion

AI empowers businesses to expand into new markets by providing insights into consumer preferences and cultural nuances. Sentiment analysis, another AI application, helps businesses understand the preferences and opinions of consumers in different markets. Companies gain valuable insights into consumer sentiment by analyzing social media data, customer reviews, and other sources, allowing them to tailor their products and marketing strategies.

Competitive Advantage

Companies that effectively leverage AI gain a significant competitive advantage. AI helps businesses differentiate themselves by offering innovative products and services, improving customer experience, and reducing costs. Personalized AI marketing campaigns can achieve higher conversion rates, increase customer loyalty, and enhance brand reputation.

Global Collaboration

AI facilitates global collaboration by enabling teams to work remotely and communicate effectively across time zones and cultures. AI-powered translation tools break down language barriers, foster seamless communication and collaboration between teams from different countries, and enable businesses to reach a wider global audience. This can lead to improved productivity, innovation, and knowledge sharing.

AI and Individuals

Increased Productivity

AI augments human capabilities, enabling individuals to work more efficiently and productively. For example, imagine a radiologist tasked with analyzing hundreds of medical images for potential abnormalities. AI-powered image recognition software can assist by quickly identifying potential areas of concern, allowing the radiologist to focus their attention on the most critical cases. This not only accelerates the diagnostic process but also reduces the risk of human error, ultimately improving patient care and freeing up valuable time for more nuanced analyses.

By automating routine tasks, AI frees workers to focus on more complex and creative endeavors, increasing job satisfaction and productivity.

New Opportunities

AI presents new avenues for entrepreneurship and innovation. Individuals can use AI to develop innovative products and services or start an AI-powered business. For example, entrepreneurs can leverage AI to create personalized learning platforms, develop AI-powered healthcare solutions, or develop new applications for various industries.

Ethical Considerations

Bias and Fairness

AI algorithms can be biased if trained on biased data, which may lead to discriminatory outcomes. To avoid this bias, AI systems need to be trained on diverse and representative data. Also, companies need to implement measures to detect and mitigate bias.

Privacy and Security

AI raises concerns about data privacy and security. Businesses must implement robust measures to protect sensitive data and prevent unauthorized access. This includes obtaining informed consent from individuals, complying with data privacy regulations, and investing in solid cybersecurity measures.

Job Displacement

The potential for job displacement due to AI automation necessitates careful consideration and planning. Governments and businesses need to collaborate to develop policies and programs that support workers who may be affected by automation, such as retraining programs and social safety nets.

While AI automation leads to job displacement in some sectors, it also creates new job opportunities. To capitalize on the opportunities, individuals must learn to utilize AI and develop skills complementing AI, such as critical thinking, creativity, complex problem-solving, and adaptability.

CASE STUDY: NETFLIX—THE POWER OF AI-DRIVEN PERSONALIZATION

The global streaming giant Netflix has revolutionized the entertainment industry through its innovative use of AI. One key factor behind Netflix's success is its ability to deliver highly personalized recommendations to its users.

Netflix's AI algorithms analyze vast amounts of data, including user viewing history, ratings, search queries, and interactions with the platform. By identifying patterns and preferences, these algorithms can accurately predict which movies and TV shows users will enjoy. Netflix's AI-powered recommendation system provides several key benefits:

- **Increased user engagement:** By providing personalized recommendations, Netflix engages users and makes them want to return for more. Users who find content they enjoy are more likely to spend more time on the platform.

- **Improved customer satisfaction:** Personalized recommendations help users discover new shows and movies they might not have otherwise considered. This leads to increased satisfaction and loyalty.
- **Enhanced content discovery:** Netflix's AI algorithms help users discover hidden gems or niche content that they might not have found on their own, leading to a more diverse and enriching viewing experience.
- **Optimized content strategy:** By understanding user preferences, Netflix informs its content strategy and makes data-driven decisions about which shows and movies to produce or acquire.

Netflix's success in leveraging AI for personalization has inspired other companies in the entertainment industry and beyond. As AI advances, we can expect to see even more innovative and personalized experiences in the future.

CASE STUDY: IBM WATSON—A VERSATILE AI PLATFORM

IBM Watson, a powerful AI platform, has demonstrated versatility across various industries and applications. One of its most notable areas of impact is in the healthcare sector, where it is revolutionizing medical diagnosis and treatment. IBM Watson Health leverages advanced machine learning algorithms to analyze vast medical data including patient records, clinical trials, and research literature. By identifying patterns and correlations in this data, IBM Watson helps healthcare providers develop personalized treatment plans tailored to individual patients' needs.

Here are some of the key benefits to the healthcare sector of using IBM Watson Health:

- **Improved diagnosis:** Watson assists doctors in diagnosing complex medical conditions by analyzing patient data and identifying potential diagnoses that may have otherwise been overlooked.
- **Personalized treatment plans:** By understanding a patient's unique medical history and genetic makeup, IBM Watson helps develop personalized treatment plans that are more likely to be effective than those created by healthcare professionals.
- **Reduced costs:** IBM Watson helps reduce healthcare costs by streamlining processes, improving efficiency, and preventing medical errors.
- **Drug discovery:** IBM Watson can be used to accelerate drug discovery by analyzing vast amounts of scientific data to identify potential drug targets and develop new treatments.

In addition to healthcare, IBM Watson has applications in various other industries, including financial services, customer service, and language translation. For example, IBM Watson powers chatbots that interact with customers in natural language, providing personalized assistance and support. IBM Watson represents a significant advancement in AI and has the potential to transform industries and improve people's lives.

As AI continues to evolve, we expect to see even more innovative and impactful applications of this powerful technology. Developing AI literacy, investing in AI technologies, considering ethical implications, and staying informed about AI trends are essential steps to prepare for the future of work. By proactively addressing these factors, you can thrive in the AI-driven era.

DIGITAL DIVIDE

While the number of internet users (whether through a smartphone or computer) rapidly increases throughout the world, there is still a significant number of people who do not have access to these technologies. The digital divide, or the gap between those with and those without access to technology, has significant business implications. It is important for businesses to educate themselves about the demographics of their customers, consider their access to technology, and plan accordingly.

The digital divide can hinder economic development and create social inequalities. Businesses must consider the digital divide and work to ensure everyone who would benefit has access to the tools and resources needed to participate in the digital economy.

An example of technology that has the potential to significantly decrease the digital divide is the Starlink satellite system created by SpaceX, which provides internet access to remote locations.

TALENT ACQUISITION AND DEVELOPMENT

The skills needed to succeed in the digital age are evolving rapidly. In addition to hiring new digitally skilled talent, businesses must invest in upskilling their employees through training and development in areas such as data analytics, AI, cybersecurity, and digital marketing skills to ensure employees have access to the skills they need to succeed.

CYBERSECURITY

Businesses' increased reliance on digital technologies exposes them to new cybersecurity risks. Protecting sensitive data and preventing cyberattacks is a critical challenge for companies in the digital age.

Cyberattacks lead to financial losses, reputational damage, and operational disruptions. Here are some examples of noteworthy cyberattacks and some lessons we can learn from them.

UnitedHealth's Technology Unit (2024)

The hack at UnitedHealth's technology unit, Change Healthcare, compromised the personal information of 100 million individuals, making it the largest healthcare data breach to date in the United States. Hackers, known as the "BlackCat" group, stole sensitive data, including patient diagnoses, treatment information, and Social Security numbers.

This breach significantly disrupted claims processing, impacting patients and healthcare providers nationwide. UnitedHealth incurred substantial costs, including billions of dollars in loans to affected providers and expenses related to notifying impacted individuals.

SolarWinds Hack (2020)

This sophisticated and highly impactful cyberattack targeted SolarWinds, a Texas-based software company that provides IT management tools to thousands of organizations worldwide, including government agencies, Fortune 500 companies, and critical infrastructure providers.

Hackers infiltrated SolarWinds's software supply chain by inserting malicious code into updates for its Orion platform. This code, known as "Sunburst," allowed attackers to access organizations' internal networks using the compromised software. The attack, believed to have originated from Russia, compromised numerous US government agencies, including the Department of Homeland Security, the Department of Commerce, and the Department of Energy, as well as private companies like Microsoft and Cisco. The SolarWinds hack was significant for several reasons:

- **Sophistication:** The attack demonstrated a high level of sophistication and operational security, highlighting the evolving capabilities of state-sponsored cyber actors.
- **Widespread impact:** The compromise of SolarWinds's software allowed attackers to gain access to a vast number of organizations, potentially enabling them to steal valuable data, conduct espionage, and disrupt critical operations.
- **Supply chain risk:** The attack underscored the vulnerability of software supply chains and the potential for malicious actors to exploit them to compromise numerous organizations simultaneously.

The SolarWinds hack had significant geopolitical implications and raised serious concerns about critical infrastructure security and the potential for cyberattacks to disrupt essential services.

WannaCry (2017)

This ransomware attack, also known as "Wcry" or "WanaCrypt0r 2.0," exploited a vulnerability in Microsoft Windows known as "EternalBlue." Initially developed by the US National Security Agency (NSA), this vulnerability was leaked by a hacking group called The Shadow Brokers. WannaCry spread rapidly across the globe, infecting hundreds of thousands of computers in more than 150 countries.

The attack crippled critical infrastructure, including hospitals, businesses, and government agencies. The UK's National Health Service (NHS) was particularly hard hit, with thousands of appointments canceled and ambulances rerouted due to disrupted computer systems. The attack highlighted the vulnerability of interconnected systems and the potential for widespread disruption when critical infrastructure is compromised.

Equifax Data Breach (2017)

This massive data breach exposed the sensitive personal information, including Social Security numbers, dates of birth, addresses, and in some cases, driver's license numbers and credit card information of more than 147 million Americans. The breach occurred due to various factors, including outdated software, insufficient security measures, and failing to address known vulnerabilities promptly.

The Equifax breach had significant consequences for individuals, including increased risk of identity theft, fraud, and financial loss. It also damaged Equifax's reputation and led to substantial financial penalties and legal repercussions.

These breaches underscore the increasing threat of cyberattacks and the critical need for robust cybersecurity measures to protect sensitive data. You can protect your business from cybersecurity threats by implementing strong security measures and educating your employees about best practices. This includes using firewalls, encryption, and strong passwords and training employees to recognize and avoid phishing scams.

DISRUPTION

Businesses must be able to adapt to change and innovate to remain competitive. Digital technologies enable businesses to disrupt traditional business models and industries. For example, the rise of ride-sharing services like Uber and Lyft, which rely on the use of smartphones, has disrupted the traditional taxi industry.

The following case studies provide additional examples of businesses that have become successful through disrupting the market with digital technologies.

CASE STUDY: THE RISE OF STREAMING SERVICES AND THE DECLINE OF PHYSICAL MUSIC SALES

In past decades, the music industry relied heavily on sales of physical CDs and records. However, the advent of digital technologies, particularly the internet and mobile devices, disrupted this model.

Companies like Spotify, Apple Music, and YouTube Music became disruptors, offering on-demand access globally to vast music libraries through streaming subscriptions.

Major record labels like Universal Music Group, Sony Music Entertainment, and Warner Music Group initially resisted the shift, viewing digital music as a threat to their revenue streams. Sales of CDs and records plummeted as consumers embraced the convenience and affordability of streaming services. But while initial revenue from streaming was low, it gradually increased as subscription models matured.

This industry disruption gave artists more control over their careers, with some bypassing traditional record labels to reach audiences directly through platforms like Bandcamp and Patreon. Many artists embraced digital platforms to connect with fans, build direct-to-consumer relationships, and explore new avenues for creativity and income generation.

Major record labels eventually adapted by embracing streaming, investing in their own platforms, and exploring new revenue streams like merchandise and live performances.

The rise of streaming services has significantly impacted the music industry's economic landscape. While the decline in physical music sales initially led to a decline in revenue for record labels and artists, the emergence of subscription-based streaming services created new revenue streams and fostered new models for music consumption and distribution. Streaming platforms have become the dominant mode of music consumption, generating substantial revenue for artists, labels, and the broader music ecosystem.

The music industry's experience highlights the importance of adaptability and innovation in the face of rapid technological change.

CASE STUDY: NETFLIX—A STREAMING REVOLUTION

Once a tiny mail-order DVD rental company, Netflix has transformed the entertainment industry through its innovative streaming technology. By offering a vast library of movies and TV shows on demand, Netflix disrupted the traditional cable and satellite television model and created a new way for consumers to access content.

Netflix's investment in streaming technology has been a critical driver of its success. The company's streaming platform provides a seamless user experience, allowing customers to watch their favorite shows and movies on various devices, including TVs, computers, and smartphones.

While Netflix is US-based, it has expanded globally, providing a variety of international content in many languages. According to Netflix, it has 283 million paid memberships in more than 190 countries. This international expansion has enabled Netflix to reach a massive customer base and generate significant revenue.

Netflix's use of data analytics is another critical factor in its success. The company collects and analyzes customer viewing habits, preferences, and demographic data. This data is used to personalize recommendations and tailor content offerings to individual users. By providing personalized recommendations, Netflix has increased customer engagement and satisfaction.

Despite its success, Netflix faces challenges such as increasing competition from other streaming services, rising content costs, and regulatory changes. However, the company's strong brand, innovative culture, and financial resources position it well to navigate these challenges and capitalize on future opportunities.

By leveraging streaming technology, content production, data analytics, and personalization, Netflix has revolutionized the entertainment industry and set a new standard for customer experience. As the digital landscape continues to evolve, Netflix's ability to adapt and innovate will be crucial for maintaining its leadership position.

These case studies highlight that while disruption may initially pose challenges, it creates new opportunities for businesses to transform industries and create new business models, potentially very successfully.

As businesses not only accept disruption but strategically anticipate, plan for, and initiate disruptions, they can succeed in the changing world.

KEY TAKEAWAYS

The digital transformation of global business is a powerful force that reshapes industries and creates new opportunities. By understanding the key trends, challenges, and strategies for success, companies position themselves for growth and the ability to successfully compete in the digital age.

Businesses must develop a clear and comprehensive digital strategy that aligns with business goals; invest in the latest technologies, whether cloud computing, AI, IoT, or data analytics; and prioritize cybersecurity.

Reflect on your organization's digital transformation journey. What progress have you made? What challenges do you face? How can you improve and accelerate your digital transformation effort?

Chapter 13

FUELING CREATIVITY IN A CONNECTED WORLD

Upon the global canvas of imagination, where cultures blend and boundaries blur, businesses find the inspiration to redefine their future. This chapter illuminates how a global mindset ignites creativity, empowers strategic problem-solving, and cultivates a culture where innovation knows no limits.

GLOBAL MINDSET AND INNOVATION

A global mindset cultivates a deep appreciation for diverse perspectives, driving innovation and enabling effective cross-cultural collaboration. By embracing and understanding different ways of thinking and working, businesses foster a more creative and innovative environment, which invites individuals to challenge their assumptions and develop creative solutions to complex problems.

To cultivate a truly innovative environment, organizations must strategically prioritize diversity of thought and actively recruit individuals with varied backgrounds and experiences, coupled with strong cultural intelligence. Leaders who possess high cultural intelligence are instrumental in this process, as they can forge robust relationships, establish trust, and facilitate seamless communication across cultural divides, ultimately driving inclusive and groundbreaking outcomes. By assembling diverse teams, where unique cultural insights are valued, companies can design products that resonate with a global audience. Globally astute leaders effectively guide cross-functional teams, harnessing the collective intelligence of diverse members to develop innovative solutions and achieve shared objectives.

In addition, creating an equitable and respectful workspace, encouraging experimentation and risk-taking, and promoting collaboration and knowledge sharing are essential to encouraging innovation.

Create an Equitable and Respectful Workspace

Creating a workplace that values each individual's ideas and contributions is a necessary prerequisite to fostering an innovative workplace. Leaders should model the respectful behavior they want to encourage in their employees.

It may be beneficial for leaders to use surveys and other methods to gather employee feedback to ensure all employees feel included, safe, and valued in your organization.

Leaders must also enforce strict anti-discrimination policies to protect employees from harassment and discrimination based on race, gender, sexual orientation, religion, or other characteristics.

Encourage Experimentation and Risk-Taking

Creating a culture that encourages experimentation and risk-taking, so employees feel free to try new things and take calculated risks, inevitably leads to greater innovation. Part of creating this culture of innovation is providing employees with resources and support to pursue new ideas.

For example, a multinational company that wants employees to develop innovative new products or services specifically tailored to the needs of a particular market will want to provide their staff with the resources and support needed to conduct market research and test new ideas in a limited market before launching them on a larger scale.

Promote Collaboration and Knowledge Sharing

Open communication, collaboration, and knowledge sharing are essential for innovation. Leaders with a global mindset can encourage collaboration across teams and departments and with external partners by creating opportunities for cross-functional teams to work together.

For example, a multinational company with a global research and development department might foster collaboration by creating virtual teams comprised of engineers, designers, and marketers from different countries. These teams can leverage diverse perspectives and expertise as they work together to develop new products or services. A team developing a new mobile app might include members from multiple countries, allowing them to incorporate insights and feedback from users in different regions. This cross-cultural collaboration leads to more innovative and user-centric products that resonate with a global audience.

To promote knowledge sharing, leaders can implement internal "knowledge hubs" or online platforms where employees contribute and access best practices, research findings, and market insights. Leaders encourage participation by recognizing and rewarding employees who actively share their expertise, perhaps through internal awards or public acknowledgment. Additionally, they foster a culture where asking questions and seeking help is seen as a strength, not a weakness, and where employees understand that sharing knowledge benefits the entire organization, not just individual contributors. This helps to overcome the "knowledge hoarding" mentality, fostering a collaborative environment where everyone learns and grows together.

CASE STUDY: GOOGLE—A GLOBAL MINDSET FOR INNOVATION

One key factor behind the success of technology giant Google is its solid global mindset. Google has cultivated a diverse workforce, bringing together a variety of ideas and perspectives, which has fostered a creative and innovative environment.

In addition, Google encourages employees to take risks and pursue new ideas, creating a culture of experimentation and innovation. The company provides a welcoming workplace for all and provides its employees with ample resources and support to explore and turn their ideas into reality. This freedom to innovate has led to the development of groundbreaking products and services such as Google Search, Google Maps, and Google Translate.

Google's global presence requires effective collaboration across different teams and regions. The company has implemented various initiatives to foster global cooperation, including virtual teams, international conferences, and cross-cultural training programs. These initiatives help break down barriers, promote knowledge sharing, and facilitate the development of innovative solutions.

Google's strong focus on user experience has also been a key driver of its success. The company's products and services are designed to be user-friendly, intuitive, and accessible to people from all walks of life. This focus has helped Google build a loyal customer base and establish itself as a trusted brand.

By fostering a culture of innovation and collaboration, Google has developed groundbreaking products and services that have transformed the way we live and work.

CASE STUDY: UNILEVER—A GLOBAL LEADER IN SUSTAINABLE INNOVATION

Unilever, a multinational consumer goods company with a portfolio of successful brands, is a prime example of a company that has successfully leveraged a global mindset to foster innovation. Here are some of the ways Unilever excels at innovation:

- Unilever has established global innovation centers and encourages cross-functional collaboration and knowledge sharing to foster the development of new ideas and products. This collaborative approach led to the creation of successful brands such as Dove, Hellmann's, and Lipton.
- Unilever is a leader in sustainability. The company works toward ambitious goals to reduce its ecological footprint, including reducing greenhouse gas emissions, water usage, and waste. Unilever has also developed a range of sustainable products, such as plastic-free packaging and plant-based alternatives to meat.
- Unilever has implemented programs to empower women, improve livelihoods, and address social issues.

Unilever's success demonstrates how a global mindset can foster innovation, drive sustainable growth, and be a powerful force for positive change. Companies adopting a similar innovative approach will be well positioned to thrive as the global landscape evolves.

KEY TAKEAWAYS

A global mindset is crucial for fostering innovation and creativity in today's interconnected world. By understanding different cultures, perspectives, and trends, individuals can develop new ideas, solve complex problems, and create a more innovative organization.

To foster innovation, businesses should create an equitable and respectful workplace, encourage experimentation and risk-taking, and promote collaboration and knowledge sharing.

Reflect on your organization's culture and how it fosters or hinders innovation. What steps can your organization take to encourage creativity and innovation?

Chapter 14

GLOBAL ENTREPRENEURSHIP

Entrepreneurship transcends geographical boundaries in today's hyperconnected world, offering unprecedented opportunities for innovation, growth, and impact. Unlike traditional business models confined to local markets, global entrepreneurship empowers individuals to leverage the interconnectedness of our planet, accessing international markets, tapping into diverse talent pools, and driving innovation through exchanging ideas across cultures. Successfully navigating this dynamic and complex landscape requires a unique blend of entrepreneurial spirit, cultural sensitivity, and a deep understanding of the global market.

This chapter explores international entrepreneurship's exciting opportunities and challenges, providing insights and strategies for aspiring global entrepreneurs to thrive in this ever-evolving world.

OPPORTUNITIES FOR GLOBAL ENTREPRENEURS

Global entrepreneurship, compared to entrepreneurship in a single, local market, offers many unique opportunities. Here are a few.

Access to a Global Market

Global entrepreneurs have the ability to tap into a vast international market, including new and emerging markets. Such access can lead to significant growth and profitability as businesses scale their operations and increase revenue.

Access to a Diverse Talent Pool

Global entrepreneurs have access to a worldwide, diverse talent pool. Assembling a diverse team can help companies develop innovative products and services, gain a competitive advantage, and better understand their customers' needs.

Additionally, team members with international backgrounds provide invaluable insights into specific markets, leading to more targeted and successful global strategies.

Cost Savings

Global entrepreneurs have the opportunity to establish offices in countries with lower labor, property, and other costs, so more funds can be used to scale and improve the business and increase profitability. This is particularly beneficial for companies in industries such as manufacturing and customer service.

Cultural Exchange

Global entrepreneurship fosters cultural exchange, leading to new partnerships and opportunities. By operating in different cultures, businesses gain valuable insights and perspectives that will help them innovate and succeed.

CHALLENGES OF GLOBAL ENTREPRENEURSHIP

Cultural Differences

Understanding and adapting to cultural differences is challenging for some global entrepreneurs. It can be difficult to understand different business practices, communication styles, and values. Failure to understand cultural differences can lead to misunderstandings, miscommunications, and even business failures.

Language Barriers

Language barriers make communicating with customers, suppliers, and partners in foreign markets difficult, which sometimes hinders business operations and limits growth opportunities.

Regulatory Hurdles

Navigating the complex regulatory environments in different countries can be challenging. This includes obtaining visas, permits, and licenses and complying with local employment laws, tax laws, and other regulations.

Financing

Accessing financing for a global business may be difficult, especially in emerging markets. Investors may hesitate to invest in companies operating in unfamiliar markets that they think will expose them to political and economic risks.

Risk Management

Global entrepreneurs may be exposed to various risks, including political instability, economic fluctuations, and currency fluctuations.

STRATEGIES FOR SUCCESSFUL GLOBAL ENTREPRENEURSHIP

By maintaining a global mindset and employing the following strategies, global entrepreneurs will maximize the success of their businesses.

Market Research

When establishing an international company, it is essential to conduct thorough market research in order to understand the needs and preferences of customers in your target markets. This market research will help you to differentiate your products and services to meet local demand.

Local Partnerships

Among other benefits, partnering with local businesses and organizations will help you gain insights into the local market and build strategic relationships. Having local partners will help you successfully navigate the complexities of the local business environment and avoid common pitfalls.

Cultural Sensitivity

Demonstrate cultural sensitivity and respect for local customs and traditions. This will help you build trust with local partners and customers.

Effective Communication

Develop strong communication skills and communicate effectively with people from different cultures. This includes understanding different communication styles and using appropriate language.

Risk Management

Develop a risk management plan to mitigate business risks. This may involve diversifying your supply chain, purchasing insurance, and developing contingency plans.

Financing

Develop a sound financial plan and explore financing options such as venture capital, angel investors, and crowdfunding.

Airbnb was founded in the US in 2008 and began expanding internationally in 2011. The platform allows individuals to rent out their homes, apartments, or spare rooms to travelers, providing a more affordable and personalized alternative to traditional hotels. It has revolutionized the hospitality industry by connecting travelers with unique accommodation options worldwide.

Airbnb's success can be attributed to several factors:

- Airbnb challenged the traditional hotel industry by offering a peer-to-peer accommodation platform. This model disrupted the market and provided travelers with more affordable and flexible options.
- Airbnb has a global reach—it operates in more than 190 countries, making it one of the largest accommodation providers in the world. This international presence has allowed Airbnb to tap into diverse markets and cater to the needs of travelers from all walks of life.
- Airbnb's user-friendly, technology-driven platform and mobile app have made it easy for travelers to book accommodations and for hosts to manage their listings. The company invests in technology to ensure the safety and security of its users.
- Airbnb fosters a sense of community among its users by allowing travelers to connect with other travelers and hosts, sharing experiences and recommendations.

CASE STUDY: SPOTIFY—ENTREPRENEURSHIP IN THE MUSIC INDUSTRY

Spotify, a Swedish music streaming service, has transformed how people listen to music. Created in 2006 as a small start-up, Spotify officially launched in multiple countries in 2008. Spotify now offers a vast library of songs from millions of artists, allowing users to stream them on demand. Spotify's success can be attributed to several factors:

- Spotify's user-friendly, intuitive interface and personalized recommendations make it easy for users to discover new music and create playlists.
- Spotify partners with local music labels and artists in various countries around the world, helping them appeal to a global audience. It has expanded its operations to more than 100 countries.
- Spotify has successfully expanded into the podcasting market, becoming a leading platform for podcast discovery and consumption.
- The platform offers an innovative freemium model that allows users to listen to free content with ads or subscribe to a premium paid service that includes ad-free listening and other features.

Airbnb and Spotify are examples of successful global entrepreneurial businesses that have disrupted their respective industries. These companies have demonstrated the potential for entrepreneurs to create innovative and scalable worldwide businesses.

KEY TAKEAWAYS

Global entrepreneurship presents businesses with many opportunities and challenges. Successful global entrepreneurs must deeply understand their target markets, build relationships with local partners, demonstrate cultural sensitivity, communicate effectively, develop effective risk management strategies, and develop a sound financial plan.

Reflect on your entrepreneurial aspirations. What are your goals for your business? What challenges do you anticipate facing as you expand your business globally? How can you prepare for these challenges and seize the opportunities presented by global entrepreneurship?

SECTION 4

CASE STUDIES AND FUTURE PERSPECTIVES

Chapter 15

GLOBAL MINDSET LEADER CASE STUDIES

In the current business environment, it's more important than ever for leaders to employ a global mindset. In this chapter we will examine nine global leaders who have been successful in part because of their global mindset:

Tedros Adhanom Ghebreyesus

Anousheh Ansari

Melinda Gates

The Dalai Lama

Jack Ma

Sundar Pichai

Howard Schultz

Ricardo Semler

Malala Yousafzai

We will discuss the characteristics of these individuals, the global impact they have made, and what lessons we can learn from their experiences.

TEDROS ADHANOM GHEBREYESUS: DIRECTOR-GENERAL OF THE WORLD HEALTH ORGANIZATION

Ethiopian Tedros Adhanom Ghebreyesus's dedication to improving global health and his experience working in diverse healthcare systems have made him an asset to the World Health Organization (WHO). He has demonstrated cultural sensitivity as he has played a crucial role in responding to global health emergencies such as the COVID-19 pandemic. And seeking to improve the health of peoples throughout the world, he has advocated for universal health coverage. As Ethiopia's minister of health from 2005 to 2012, Dr. Ghebreyesus led a comprehensive reform of the country's health system, built on the foundation of universal health coverage and provision of services to all people, even in the most remote areas.

Under his leadership, Ethiopia expanded its health infrastructure, developed innovative health financing mechanisms, and expanded its health workforce. A significant component of the reforms he spearheaded was creating a primary healthcare extension program that deployed 40,000 female health workers throughout the country. This resulted in roughly a 60 percent reduction in child and maternal mortality compared to levels from the year 2000.

Before he was elected director-general of the WHO, Dr. Ghebreyesus held many leadership positions in global health, including as chair of the Global Fund to Fight AIDS, Tuberculosis, and Malaria; chair of the Roll Back Malaria Partnership; and cochair of the Partnership for Maternal, Newborn, and Child Health Board.

Dr. Ghebreyesus's work demonstrates the difference one globally-minded leader, committed to making the world a better place, can make.

ANOUSHEH ANSARI: IRANIAN-AMERICAN ENTREPRENEUR AND SPACE TOURIST

Anousheh Ansari embodies a true global mindset. She was born in Iran and immigrated with her family to the United States as a teenager. Her journey, from immigrating to the United States to becoming the first female space tourist, exemplifies the power of embracing diversity and an international perspective.

Ansari's experience as an immigrant instilled in her a deep appreciation for different cultures and perspectives. By navigating a new country and adapting to a new environment, she gained a unique understanding of cultural differences and the importance of inclusivity.

As the first female space tourist, Ansari's journey to the International Space Station in 2005 marked a historic milestone. Her participation in the Soyuz mission, an international collaboration, underscored the importance of global cooperation in advancing scientific endeavors. This experience highlighted the value of diverse perspectives and the power of international cooperation in achieving ambitious goals.

Ansari's entrepreneurial journey began in 2006 when she cofounded Prodea Systems, a telecommunications company that she later sold to British Telecom. With the proceeds from this sale, she established the X Prize Foundation, a nonprofit organization dedicated to incentivizing innovation and technological breakthroughs. Through the X Prize Foundation, Ansari actively promotes innovation and technological advancement on a global scale. The X Prize Foundation fosters international collaboration among scientists, engineers, and entrepreneurs by incentivizing groundbreaking solutions to global challenges.

In addition, Ansari's advocacy for STEM education and women's empowerment in science and technology reflects her commitment to fostering a globally-minded and inclusive future. By inspiring young people from all backgrounds to pursue STEM careers, she contributes to a more diverse and innovative workforce.

Anousheh Ansari's life and career demonstrate how a global mindset can drive innovation, foster collaboration, and positively impact the world. Her journey exemplifies the power of embracing diversity, overcoming challenges, and pursuing ambitious goals with a global perspective.

MELINDA GATES:
A FORCE FOR GLOBAL GOOD

American Melinda Gates, cofounder of the Bill & Melinda Gates Foundation, is a leader dedicated to improving people's lives worldwide. With her deep understanding of the challenges faced by developing countries, Gates has spearheaded innovative solutions and invested billions of dollars in initiatives spanning education, healthcare, and economic development.

Gates's philanthropic journey began when she and her then-husband, Bill Gates, established their foundation in the early 1990s. The foundation's mission is to improve the health and well-being of people worldwide, primarily in developing countries. Melinda Gates has been instrumental in shaping the foundation's strategic direction and guiding its philanthropic efforts.

One of Gates's key areas of focus is global health. She has championed initiatives to combat diseases such as malaria, tuberculosis, and polio and has advocated for increased access to vaccines and essential healthcare services. Gates has been a strong advocate for women's health and empowerment, recognizing women's critical role in the health and development of their communities.

Gates also invests heavily in education. She believes education is a powerful tool for breaking the cycle of poverty and empowering individuals. The Gates Foundation supports initiatives to improve education quality, increase access to education, and promote gender equality in education.

Gates's philanthropic work has extended to economic development. She supports initiatives to promote agricultural development, financial inclusion, and entrepreneurship in developing countries. By investing in these areas, Gates aims to help people lift themselves out of poverty and improve their livelihoods.

Melinda Gates's commitment to global philanthropy and her deep understanding of the challenges facing developing countries have made her a respected figure on the world stage. Her work has inspired countless individuals and organizations to join the fight for a more just and equitable world. Gates's legacy will continue to have a lasting impact on the lives of millions of people around the globe.

THE DALAI LAMA: A CHAMPION OF DIALOGUE

The fourteenth Dalai Lama, Tibetan Buddhist monk Tenzin Gyatso, is a revered spiritual leader and Nobel Peace Prize laureate. He has consistently advocated for a world characterized by harmony, compassion, and understanding. His unwavering belief in the power of dialogue has made him a beacon of hope in a world often divided by conflict and misunderstanding.

In the face of twenty-first-century challenges and complexities, the Dalai Lama emphasizes the imperative for open and respectful dialogue between people from different cultures, religions, and backgrounds. He firmly believes that the world's pressing problems, such as climate change, inequality, and conflict, can only be addressed through mutual understanding, cooperation, and a shared commitment to the common good.

The Dalai Lama's message of dialogue is rooted in his deep understanding of human nature and his belief in the inherent goodness of all people. He has spent decades fostering interfaith, cross-cultural dialogue and promoting peaceful coexistence between communities. His tireless efforts to bridge divides and foster understanding have earned him widespread respect and admiration worldwide.

In addition to his advocacy for open dialogue, the Dalai Lama emphasizes the importance of compassion, kindness, and ethical conduct. He believes that cultivating these qualities within us creates a more harmonious and compassionate world. His teachings on ethics, mindfulness, and inner peace have inspired millions of people to live more meaningful and fulfilling lives.

The Dalai Lama's message is particularly relevant in today's interconnected world. As globalization has brought people from different cultures and backgrounds into closer contact, it is more important than ever to foster understanding, respect, and cooperation. By embracing the values taught by the Dalai Lama, we can create a more peaceful, just, and sustainable world for all.

JACK MA: A VISIONARY LEADER SHAPING THE GLOBAL ECONOMY

Chinese Jack Ma, Alibaba's visionary founder, has played a pivotal role in shaping the global e-commerce landscape. Ma recognized the internet's potential to revolutionize commerce and connect businesses with consumers on a global scale, and with this vision in mind, he founded Alibaba in 1999 to connect Chinese businesses with international buyers. His entrepreneurial spirit and innovative approach to business have propelled Alibaba to become one of the world's largest and most influential technology companies.

One of Ma's key strategies was to focus on innovation and customer-centricity. Alibaba's platforms, such as Taobao and Tmall, offer a user-friendly experience, a vast selection of products, and competitive prices. Ma also recognized the importance of building solid relationships with local businesses and providing them with the tools and resources needed to succeed online. Alibaba's commitment to innovation led to the development of groundbreaking products and services such as Alipay, a popular mobile payment platform, and AliExpress, a global online marketplace. These innovations helped Alibaba expand its reach and attract a growing customer base.

Ma's entrepreneurial spirit and global vision have significantly impacted the global economy. Alibaba has created millions of jobs, empowered small businesses, and promoted economic development in China and beyond. Ma's leadership has also inspired countless entrepreneurs and innovators around the world.

Ma is also a prominent philanthropist. He founded the Jack Ma Foundation, which focuses on education, healthcare, and environmental sustainability. Ma's commitment to social responsibility has further solidified his reputation as a global leader.

Jack Ma's legacy as a visionary entrepreneur and global leader will continue to inspire future generations. His focus on innovation, customer-centricity, and building strong partnerships has transformed the e-commerce landscape and left an indelible mark on the global economy.

SUNDAR PICHAI: CEO OF ALPHABET INC. AND GOOGLE

Indian-born American Sundar Pichai, a visionary leader with a keen eye for innovation, has been at the helm of Alphabet Inc. and its subsidiary, Google, since 2015. His strategic guidance has been instrumental in driving the company's growth and success on a global scale. Pichai's unwavering commitment to innovation has fostered a culture of creativity and experimentation within Google, leading to the development of groundbreaking products and services that have revolutionized various industries.

Pichai's emphasis on user experience has been a cornerstone of Google's philosophy. He understands that the company's success hinges on delivering products that are intuitive and accessible and that meet the evolving needs of its diverse user base. Under Pichai's leadership, Google has consistently prioritized user-centric design, resulting in products like Android, Chrome, and Google Search, that have become ubiquitous in people's lives.

Furthermore, Pichai has been a champion of treating all employees equally and encouraging diverse thinking within Google. He recognizes that a diverse workforce, where everyone's perspectives and insights are valued, is able to innovate and create products that resonate with a global audience. Pichai's initiatives to create an inclusive workplace have helped Google attract and retain top talent worldwide.

Pichai's leadership has propelled Google to new heights and solidified its position as a leading technology company. Pichai's example of visionary leadership, combined with his focus on innovation, user experience, and diversity, has positioned Google to continue shaping the future of technology and driving positive changes in the world and will continue to inspire future leaders.

HOWARD SCHULTZ: FOSTERING GLOBAL COMMUNITY THROUGH STARBUCKS

American Howard Schultz, the former CEO of Starbucks, is renowned for his global mindset and ability to create a sense of international community. Schultz's vision and leadership was instrumental in transforming Starbucks from a regional coffee shop chain into a global brand with a presence in more than 70 countries.

One of Schultz's critical strategies for fostering a global community was creating a welcoming and inclusive environment for Starbucks customers and employees worldwide. Under Schultz's leadership, Starbucks made a conscious effort to hire a diverse workforce that reflected the diversity of its customers. Starbucks' sensitivity to local demographics has helped them build strong relationships with local communities and create a sense of belonging for customers from all walks of life.

In addition, Schultz focused on creating a "third place"—a place apart from home and work—where people can gather and connect. Starbucks stores are designed to be comfortable and inviting, providing a space where people can socialize, work, or relax. This concept of a "third place" helped Starbucks become a popular destination for people worldwide.

Schultz's global mindset also extended to his advocacy for social justice and environmental sustainability. Starbucks has been a leader in fair trade sourcing and has implemented various initiatives to reduce its environmental impact. These efforts helped strengthen Starbucks's reputation as a socially responsible company and have contributed to its success in global markets.

Howard Schultz's global mindset and focus on community and social responsibility provide a great example to emulate for future leaders who want to make the world a better place.

RICARDO SEMLER: A PIONEER OF EMPLOYEE EMPOWERMENT

Brazilian Ricardo Semler, the former CEO of the multinational company Semco Partners, is renowned for his innovative management style that empowers employees with autonomy and decision-making authority. This approach played a crucial role in Semco's global success, fostering a culture of innovation, adaptability, and employee engagement.

Semler believed that traditional hierarchical management structures were outdated and stifled creativity. He sought to create a more democratic and empowering workplace where employees felt valued, motivated, and invested in the company's success. To achieve this, Semler implemented a series of radical changes, including introducing a profit-sharing system that incentivized employees to work harder and smarter, and open book management, sharing financial information with all employees, empowering them to make informed decisions and take ownership of their work. He also encouraged employees to form self-managed teams that had the autonomy to set their own goals, make decisions, and manage their own work. And he allowed employees to set their own schedules and work from home or other locations.

These innovative practices fostered trust, collaboration, and empowerment culture at Semco. Employees felt valued and motivated and were more likely to take initiative, innovate, and contribute to the company's success. This culture of innovation and adaptability enabled Semco to thrive in diverse markets and remain competitive in a rapidly changing business environment.

Semler's approach to management has been widely praised and studied by other companies seeking to create more engaged and productive workforces.

MALALA YOUSAFZAI: A BEACON OF HOPE FOR GLOBAL EDUCATION

Malala Yousafzai, the Pakistani activist for female education, has become a global icon for her unwavering commitment to empowering girls and promoting education.

Yousafzai's journey began at a young age when she started a blog documenting the Taliban's takeover of her hometown, Swat Valley, and the restrictions the Taliban imposed on girls' education. Her blog gained international attention, and she became a symbol of resistance against the Taliban's oppressive regime.

In 2012, Yousafzai was shot in the head by Taliban militants who sought to assassinate her because of her activism. Her miraculous recovery is a testament to her resilience and determination.

Since her recovery, Yousafzai has continued to advocate in countries around the world for girls' education. She has addressed world leaders, spoken at international conferences, and published a critically acclaimed memoir, *I Am Malala*. Her courage, resilience, and powerful message about the importance of education for all has resonated with and inspired audiences worldwide. She has become a symbol of hope and resilience, inspiring people of all ages and backgrounds to stand up for their rights. Yousafzai's story is a powerful reminder of the importance of speaking out against injustice and inequality and the impact one individual can have on the world.

KEY TAKEAWAYS

The leaders discussed in this chapter have shown that it is possible to create a more just and equitable world and succeed in the global economy through adopting a global mindset and respecting and valuing different cultures. They have all faced challenges, but they have overcome them by being open-minded, adaptable, and committed to providing opportunities for people around the world.

Reflect on your organization's cross-cultural leadership practices. Are your leaders visionary and innovative, and do they value other cultures? Do they inspire your team and work to create a better world? How can you improve your organization's global mindset and ability to lead effectively across cultures?

Chapter 16

THE FUTURE OF GLOBAL BUSINESS

The future of global business is increasingly uncertain and volatile. Technological advancements, changing consumer preferences, and political instability are just a few factors that will continue to shape the global business environment.

Successful global leadership requires a multifaceted approach to leadership, encompassing cultural intelligence, cross-cultural collaboration, and a keen awareness of global trends and developments.

Global mindset leaders who appreciate different cultures and develop agile and adaptable organizations will be key players in the future of global business.

AGILITY AND ADAPTABILITY

Agility and adaptability are distinct yet interconnected concepts crucial for navigating the dynamic landscape of the modern business world. *Agility* refers to the capacity for rapid response and effective action in the face of change. Agile organizations possess a keen awareness of their environments, proactively identifying and responding to emerging trends, market shifts, and unforeseen challenges. Agility is aided by flexible structures, efficient processes, and a culture that embraces experimentation and rapid iteration.

Adaptability, while closely related to agility, focuses on the ability to learn, evolve, and grow in response to change. Adaptable organizations continually learn from their experiences—both successes and failures—and leverage these insights to refine their strategies, improve their products and services, and enhance their overall performance. Adaptability is aided by a willingness to embrace change, experiment with new ideas, and continually adapt to the evolving needs of the market and their customers.

In essence, agility is about reacting swiftly to change, and adaptability is about learning and growing from those experiences to improve and thrive in the changing environment. Both are essential for long-term success in today's rapidly evolving business world. As said by Jim Collins, coauthor of the bestselling books *Built to Last* and *Good to Great*, "Good is the enemy of great." Developing a global mindset and being agile and adaptable are essential for *good* leaders to become *great* leaders who then help their organizations become agile and adaptable.

There are many benefits to being agile and adaptable as an organization. Here are a few:

- **Increased customer satisfaction:** Agile and adaptable organizations quickly identify and respond to customer needs, leading to increased customer satisfaction and loyalty.
- **Improved financial performance:** As these organizations quickly and effectively adjust to change, they are likely to maximize profits.

- **Increased innovation:** As agile, adaptable organizations constantly learn and grow, they create an innovative culture where positive changes are encouraged and welcomed. Businesses that adapt to change quickly and effectively are able to stay ahead of the competition and increase the likelihood they will be successful in the future.

Anticipating Change

It's important that you don't just sit back and wait for change to happen to your organization, but rather be proactive and look for ways to anticipate change.

One way businesses can anticipate trends and other developments is conducting regular market research. Businesses can also use data analytics to track customer behavior and identify potential changes in demand. Additionally, companies can build relationships with key stakeholders, suppliers, and customers to stay current on industry news and trends.

By staying informed about technological advancements, evolving consumer preferences, geopolitical shifts, and trends relating to sustainability, leaders can anticipate future challenges and opportunities and proactively adapt, positioning their organizations for success in the dynamic global marketplace. This may involve changing product offerings, modifying pricing structures, expanding into new markets, or changing your business model or strategy.

Here is a more detailed discussion of the areas where being agile and adaptable is advantageous for businesses now and in the future.

New Trends and Technologies

New technologies can be expensive and time-consuming to implement, but they create opportunities for businesses and improve the way businesses operate. For example, companies can use new technologies to improve customer service, automate tasks, and create new products and services.

Businesses that invest in training and development to stay up to date on the latest trends and technologies and that adopt new technologies quickly will gain a competitive advantage. As discussed in chapter 12, some of the most promising new technologies include AI, big data, and cloud computing. These technologies have the potential to revolutionize business operations, and businesses that adopt them early on will reduce costs and improve efficiency.

The changing nature of work is also leading to a more flexible workforce. More and more people are working remotely or on a contract basis, creating new business challenges and opportunities.

New Markets and Changing Consumer Preferences

The rapid growth of the global economy is creating new markets for businesses to enter. And consumer preferences are changing rapidly as people become more demanding and informed about their choices, creating business opportunities.

Agile, adaptable organizations always keep their customers' needs in mind—businesses must adapt their products and services to meet changing preferences or they will lose market share. Businesses that offer products and services tailored to the needs of a growing global middle class will be well positioned for success.

Political Instability

Agile, adaptable organizations are able to weather the economic uncertainty and disruption brought about by political instability. They take steps to limit their exposure to risk. For example, to mitigate the risk of political instability in any one country, they may choose to operate in multiple countries. Agile, adaptable organizations are able to adapt to political unrest and continue operating and growing.

The Increasing Demand for Sustainability

Consumers are becoming more aware of their purchases' environmental impact and are more likely to demand sustainable products and services. This growing awareness presents both challenges and opportunities for businesses. Companies that can adapt to this evolving consumer demand with agility, and embrace sustainable practices and integrate them into their core business strategies, will be well positioned for long-term success.

Businesses can become more sustainable by using recycled materials, reducing their energy consumption, and developing products that are made to last. By embracing sustainable practices, businesses not only reduce their environmental impact but also enhance their brand image, attract environmentally conscious consumers, and gain a competitive advantage in the marketplace.

AGILE AND ADAPTABLE COMPANIES

Here are some examples of successful agile and adaptable companies.

Amazon

Amazon's journey from an online bookstore to a global e-commerce giant is a prime example of agility and adaptability. The company continually innovates and expands its product offerings, from cloud computing services (Amazon Web Services) to AI (Alexa) and logistics. Amazon's ability to anticipate market trends and consumer needs has allowed it to stay ahead of competitors and maintain its position as a market leader.

Apple

Apple's ability to anticipate consumer preferences and adapt its product offerings has been a cornerstone of its success. The company's transition from personal computers to mobile devices, such as the iPhone and iPad, revolutionized the tech industry. Apple's focus on innovation, design, and user experience has allowed it to maintain a loyal customer base and stay ahead of competitors.

BioWare

BioWare initially focused on creating medical education software, including a gastroenterology patient simulator. The founders, who were avid gamers, soon transitioned toward video game development. BioWare went on to become a powerhouse in the gaming industry, creating critically acclaimed franchises such as Baldur's Gate, Mass Effect, and Dragon Age. This transformation showcases how the company successfully leveraged the founders' programming skills and passion for gaming to pivot from medical software to creating some of the most influential role-playing games in the industry.

Caterpillar

The world's leading construction and mining equipment manufacturer has transformed into a hardware and software company. Caterpillar now leverages AI and digital twins to predict maintenance, anticipate the need for part replacements, and assist in automation. This transformation is expected to significantly contribute to their service revenues, with forecasts of $28 billion by 2025, doubling from $14 billion in 2016.

LEGO

LEGO faced near-bankruptcy in the early 2000s but transformed its business model by expanding into video games, movies, and theme parks while maintaining its core product line. This adaptation helped LEGO become one of the world's most valuable toy companies.

Philips

Originally only a lighting and electronics company, Philips pivoted to become a leader in healthcare technology. It developed the HealthSuite Digital Platform (HSDP) and CDP Medical, offering cloud-based healthcare solutions. Philips has also embraced cocreation through HealthSuite Labs, collaborating with stakeholders to develop innovative healthcare solutions.

KEY TAKEAWAYS

The future of global business is uncertain, but agile and adaptable organizations will be well positioned to succeed. The future belongs to companies who are willing and able to predict and adapt to change.

Reflect on how agile and adaptable your organization is. What are your strengths and weaknesses? How can your organization become more agile and adaptable?

Conclusion

A GLOBAL PERSPECTIVE

As you reach the final chapter of this book, you embark not on an ending but a new beginning. The journey you have undertaken as you have read and applied the principles within these pages has been one of profound transformation, a shift in perspective that will forever alter how you perceive and interact with the world.

You began this journey with an awareness of your own cultural identity, perhaps with a nascent understanding of the diverse tapestry of human cultures. Now, you stand at a vantage point, overlooking a landscape of rich cultural variations and equipped with the knowledge and tools to navigate its complexities. The concept of a "global mindset," once perhaps a mere phrase, now resonates with deeper meaning. You understand its essence, recognize its power, and possess the practical strategies to cultivate it within yourself and inspire it within others.

You have delved into the art of cross-cultural communication, recognizing the subtle nuances that create chasms or bridge divides. You have explored the delicate dance of trust-building, understanding the importance of empathy, respect, and genuine curiosity in forging meaningful connections across cultures. You have honed your problem-solving skills, learning to approach challenges with a multifaceted perspective, drawing upon the collective wisdom of diverse viewpoints.

No longer are you merely aware of cultural differences; you appreciate their profound influence on communication styles, decision-making processes, and interpersonal dynamics.

You understand the concepts of in-group and out-group dynamics and other subtle yet powerful forces shaping human interactions across cultures.

You have come to understand the key traits and abilities that define global leaders—individuals who possess intellectual prowess, emotional intelligence, cultural sensitivity, and a deep commitment to ethical conduct.

You are now equipped to attract, retain, and cultivate talent for your organization on a global scale, recognizing the immense value brought by a diverse workforce for fostering innovation and driving organizational success.

You understand that ethical considerations are not monolithic; they vary across cultures, demanding careful consideration and nuanced judgment.

You appreciate the intricate complexities of managing global supply chains, leveraging technology to enhance competitiveness and promote sustainability.

You are prepared to craft marketing campaigns that resonate with diverse audiences, recognizing the importance of cultural adaptation and brand localization.

You possess the insights to navigate the challenges and opportunities of emerging markets, understanding the key trends in global digitalization and their impact on business practices.

You have witnessed how a global mindset translates into effective leadership through examining the legacy of some noteworthy global leaders. And you understand that the future of international business demands agility, adaptability, and a willingness to embrace change.

As you step into your role as a cross-cultural leader, armed with this newfound knowledge and understanding, you will undoubtedly achieve remarkable success. Yet, your journey does not end here. A new chapter awaits you, focused on articulating your achievements, identifying the unique factors contributing to your success, and applying these hard-won lessons to the challenges ahead.

Our next book will illuminate this crucial step in your leadership journey, guiding you as you refine your voice, amplify your impact, and solidify your legacy as a true global leader.

We're honored to be on this journey with you and wish you continued success! If we can be of assistance, please reach out to us through the McKinney Consulting website, mckinneyconsulting.com, or on LinkedIn: Steve McKinney and Bryan McKinney.

ACKNOWLEDGMENTS

This book would not have been possible without the dedication and expertise of the remarkable team at McKinney Consulting. Every day, our colleagues work tirelessly to support our clients' success through executive search, executive coaching, and human resources consulting. Your belief in the vision for this book and its potential impact has been a constant source of motivation and inspiration.

A heartfelt thank-you to Brynn Steimle, whose keen eye, insightful feedback, and unwavering support were instrumental in shaping this book.

Finally, thank you to our readers for your commitment to learning about leadership. By choosing this book, you are investing in your own growth and in the positive transformation of those around you. We hope the insights you gain will empower you to make a meaningful difference in your organization and beyond. Wishing you all the best on your leadership journey.

BIBLIOGRAPHY

Aave. https://aave.com (accessed March 5, 2025).

Airbnb. "Newsroom: About Us." https://news.airbnb.com/about-us (accessed March 5, 2025).

Ansari, Omair, and Manahil Javaid. "Financial and Monetary Systems: Access to Credit: The Silent Issue Hampering Growth and Development in Emerging Economies." *World Economic Forum*. August 6, 2024. https://www.weforum.org/stories/2024/08/access-to-credit-slowing-growth-and-development.

Apple. "Apple Supplier Code of Conduct." January 1, 2020. https://www.apple.com/au/supplier-responsibility/pdf/Apple-Supplier-Code-of-Conduct-January.pdf.

Balte, Mark. "What You Can't See Can Hurt You – Is Your Supply Chain Really Transparent?" *Logility*. November 9, 2021. https://www.logility.com/blog/transparency-of-labor-practices-in-the-supply-chain.

Barczyk, Casimir, Charles Rarick, and Gregory Winter. "An Exploratory Study of the Cultural Values of Cameroon's Young, Elite, Urban Population: Implications for Management and International Business." *Journal of Business Diversity* 21, no. 2 (2021). http://www.na-businesspress.com/JBD/JBD21-2/1_Barczyk_RarickFinal.pdf.

Center for Creative Leadership. "Reversing a Talent Drought While Generating Millions—MARS." https://www.ccl.org/client-successes/case-studies/reversing-talent-drought-generating-millions (accessed March 5, 2025).

Chen, Michael. "Blockchain for Supply Chain: Uses and Benefits." *Oracle.* August 8, 2024. https://www.oracle.com/fi/blockchain/what-is-blockchain/blockchain-for-supply-chain.

Collins, Jim. *Good to Great*. Harper Business, 2001, p. 1.

Compound. https://compound.finance (accessed March 5, 20205.

Coulter, Josh, Erik Check, and Rachana Kathawate. "Perspectives: Using Blockchain to Drive Supply Chain Transparency. Use Cases and Future Outlook on Blockchain in Supply Chain Management." *Deloitte.* https://www2.deloitte.com/us/en/pages/operations/articles/blockchain-supply-chain-innovation.html (accessed March 5, 2025).

Dock Labs AG. "Blockchain Food Traceability: Enhancing Transparency and Safety." February 21, 2025. https://www.dock.io/post/blockchain-food-traceability.

Dunsmore, Sarah. "Unlocking Talent Development Early on and Removing Barriers for Female Leaders." *Mars.* https://www.ccl.org/client-successes/case-studies/reversing-talent-drought-generating-millionshttps://careers.mars.com/global/en/blogarticle/unlocking-talent-development-early-on-and-removing-barriers-for-female-leaders (accessed March 5, 2025).

Envoys. "The Impact of International Experience on Your Resume." February 27, 2024. https://envoys.com/schools/blog/the-impact-of-international-experience-on-your-resume.

Friedman, Thomas L. *The World is Flat: A Brief History of the Twenty-First*

Century. Farrar, Straus and Giroux, 2005.

Goldsmith, Marshall. *What Got You Here Won't Get You There: How Successful People Become Even More Successful*. Hyperion Books, 2007.

Hall, Edward T. *Beyond Culture*. Anchor Press, 1976.

Hofstede, Geert. *Culture's Consequences: International Differences in Work-Related Values*. Sage Publications, 1980.

Kanter, Rosabeth M. *World-Class: Thriving Locally in the Global Economy*. Simon & Schuster, 1995.

Kim, Albert. "How Blockchain Is Providing Sustainable Coffee." *Ledger Insights*. September 9, 2021. https://www.ledgerinsights.com/how-blockchain-is-providing-sustainable-coffee.

Kotler, Philip, and Gary Armstrong. *Principles of Marketing* (17th ed.). Pearson, 2021.

Kuchay, Bilal. "McDonald's Faces Boycott Threats in India for Serving Halal Meat." *Al Jazeera*, August 26, 2019. https://www.aljazeera.com/economy/2019/8/26/mcdonalds-faces-boycott-threats-in-india-for-serving-halal-meat.

Mars. "Learning & Development." https://careers.mars.com/global/en/learning-and-development (accessed March 5, 2025).

MasterCard. "Industry Perspectives on AI and Transaction Fraud Detection." https://b2b.mastercard.com/news-and-insights/blog/industry-perspectives-on-ai-and-transaction-fraud-detection (accessed March 5, 2025).

Netflix. "Company Profile." https://ir.netflix.net/ir-overview/profile/default.aspx (accessed March 5, 2025).

Prahalad, C.K., and Yevez L. Doz. *The Multinational Mission: Balancing Global Strategy and Local Needs*. Free Press, 1987.

Sristy, Archana. "Blockchain in the Food Supply Chain—What Does the Future Look Like?" *Walmart Global Tech*. November 30, 2021. https://tech.walmart.com/content/walmart-global-tech/en_us/blog/post/blockchain-in-the-food-supply-chain.html.

Stripe. "How Machine Learning Works for Payment Fraud Detection and Prevention." January 23, 2025. https://stripe.com/ae/resources/more/how-machine-learning-works-for-payment-fraud-detection-and-prevention.

Stryker, Cole, and Kavlakoglu, Eda. "What is Artificial intelligence (AI)?" *IBM*. August 9, 2024. https://www.ibm.com/think/topics/artificial-intelligence.

Underwood, Horace H. "Honesty vs. Loyalty: Which is More Important?" May 18, 2019. https://mckinneyconsulting.com/honesty-vs-loyalty-which-is-more-important.

Weldon, M. *The Global Mindset: Thriving in a World That's Not Your Own*. Berrett-Koehler Publishers, 2011.

World Bank Group. "Financial Inclusion Is a Key Enabler to Reducing Poverty and Boosting Prosperity." January 27, 2025. https://www.worldbank.org/en/topic/financialinclusion/overview.

World Trade Organization. "Biography: Dr Tedros Adhanom Ghebreyesus." https://www.who.int/director-general/biography (accessed April 19, 2025).

RECOMMENDED RESOURCES

The following recommended resources often provide global mindset–related insights, research, and data and analytics.

Boston Consulting Group: https://www.bcg.com

Centers for Disease Control and Prevention (CDC): https://www.cdc.gov

Council of Supply Chain Management Professionals (CSCMP): https://cscmp.org

Forbes: https://www.forbes.com

Gartner: https://www.gartner.com

Gates Foundation: https://www.gatesfoundation.org

Global Entrepreneurship Monitor (GEM): https://www.gemconsortium.org

Global Fund to Fight AIDS, Tuberculosis, and Malaria: https://www.theglobalfund.org

Global Reporting Initiative (GRI): https://www.globalreporting.org

Harvard Business Review: https://hbr.org

Interbrand: https://www.interbrand.com

International Monetary Fund: https://www.imf.org

The Joint United Nations Programme on HIV/AIDS (UNAIDS): https://www.unaids.org/en

Kwintessential: https://www.kwintessential.co.uk

McKinsey & Company: https://www.mckinsey.com

United Nations: https://www.un.org

United Nations Global Compact: https://www.unglobalcompact.org

United Nations Sustainable Development Goals: https://sdgs.un.org/goals

World Bank: https://www.worldbank.org

World Business Council for Sustainable Development (WBCSD): https://www.wbcsd.org

World Economic Forum: https://www.weforum.org

World Health Organization (WHO): https://www.who.int/about

World Trade Organization: https://www.wto.org

ABOUT THE AUTHORS

Steve McKinney

Steve McKinney has twenty-five years of experience leading professional services in Asia and over twelve years of leadership at global athletic footwear companies Adidas, Reebok, and Converse. In 2001, he established McKinney Consulting, an executive search and leadership consulting firm based in Seoul. McKinney Consulting is also a partner firm for Kestria, the world's largest executive search alliance. Steve serves on Kestria's global think tank, the Kestria Institute, which identifies emerging trends, shares innovative ideas, and provides relevant thought leadership to a diverse community of stakeholders. He is also chairman, South Korea for the Virtual Advisory Board, an organization comprising over 1,000 senior leaders worldwide, and he serves on the Asia Pacific Council of the Association of Executive Search and Leadership Consultants, a global organization with over 16,000 trusted professionals across seventy countries. Steve has authored and coauthored many articles on global leadership issues for Kestria's and McKinney's websites. In addition, Steve has been interviewed and featured in several major publications such as *Forbes, Entrepreneur, Success, Business Insider, MSN, Yahoo! News,* and others.

Steve has coached hundreds of CEOs for start-up companies and leaders for Fortune 500 and other multinational companies, and he is a keynote speaker focusing on proactive agility. He also served as the head of the Seoul Global Center for the Seoul Metropolitan Government from 2012 to 2014. In addition, Steve is a professionally trained tenor and choral conductor and holds a bachelor's degree in music education K–12, choral and band from Mars Hill University; a leadership coaching strategies certificate from Harvard University; a master certified coach credential in behavioral coaching; and a diploma in organizational neuropsychological coaching from the Behavioral Coaching Institute in New York. Steve speaks English and Korean.

Bryan McKinney

Bryan McKinney, Steve's oldest son, is a multinational business leader who has been with McKinney Consulting for fourteen years. Bryan is an expert on agility and adaptability in all business areas and was instrumental in expanding and setting up a South Korean technology and media company in California. He was raised from birth with an international mindset. His mother is Korean and his father is from the US. He studied Game Art & Design at Westwood College in Denver, Colorado, and business studies at the University of Maryland. Bryan also has a master certified coach credential in behavioral coaching and a diploma in organizational neuropsychological coaching from the Behavioral Coaching Institute in New York. Bryan speaks English, Korean, and Japanese.